TWO MINUTES
IN THE BIBLE™
for Men

∞

BOYD BAILEY

HARVEST HOUSE PUBLISHERS
EUGENE, OREGON

Cover by Left Coast Design, Portland, Oregon

TWO MINUTES IN THE BIBLE™ FOR MEN

Copyright © 2015 Boyd Bailey
Published by Harvest House Publishers
Eugene, Oregon 97402
www.harvesthousepublishers.com

Library of Congress Cataloging-in-Publication Data
Bailey, Boyd
Two minutes in the Bible for men / Boyd Bailey.
    pages cm
ISBN 978-0-7369-6532-3 (pbk.)
ISBN 978-0-7369-6533-0 (eBook)
1. Christian men—Religious life. 2. Christian men—Prayers and devotions 3. Christian life—Meditations. I. Title.
BV4528.2.B35 2015
242'.642—dc23

                                                    2015023104

Printed in the United States of America

16 17 18 19 20 21 22 23 / BP-JH / 10 9 8 7 6 5 4 3 2

To Charlie Renfroe
my mentor,
a man's man,
and most of all, God's man

To Johnny Hunt
my friend,
a man who loves men
a man with a fiery heart
for God

Introduction

Men, it's all about what God wants for us, not what we think we need for ourselves.

My struggle is striving in my own strength instead of drafting behind God, waiting in His wake. My self-reliant spirit gets in the way of the Holy Spirit's work in my life. I am learning that what I will is irrelevant unless it aligns with what God wills. Like the pull of a car with wheels out of alignment, so my prayerless choices steer me onto the rough but slippery shoulder of faithless living. I require regular listening prayer to be realigned onto Christ's purposeful path.

It's good we dream big dreams, but it's better we seek first God's kingdom and His righteousness for our lives (Matthew 6:33). We serve a big God who has big plans for us—our walk with Him, our spiritual leadership at home, our excellence at work, and our relational investments. As godly men, we plan but then submit our plans to Jesus and ask Him to order our steps. It's not enough for us to work hard and make money. We have to ask ourselves, "Why do I work?" Our noble desire is to work as for the Lord and not men. Christ is the Master over our master plan.

***

"Whatever you do, work at it with all your heart, as working for the Lord, not for human masters, since you know that you will receive an inheritance from the Lord as a reward. It is the Lord Christ you are serving" (Colossians 3:23-24).

What is your biggest insecurity? Fear of failure, a secret obsession with Internet pornography, a sense of inadequacy, or a fear of people's disapproval? These weaknesses will hold us back until we share them with loving, mature friends in the faith. Our true strength and resolve is found in the Lord. He uses His faithful servants to comfort us and to remind us of the truths of Christ, who transforms our character. We are all fellow strugglers who need each other. The more we are open and accountable to other men, the more we win!

Men, we need mentors, and we need to be mentors. We need mentors to protect us from ourselves. Older men who provide encouragement, accountability, and a proven path to follow. Pray that God will lead you to men with gray hair who admit their past mistakes, confess their current struggles, and give God glory for their successes. The Lord also calls us to mentor young men. Pouring God's blessings into the next generation is wise stewardship. Only what we give away will remain after we go to the grave. Support teachable and faithful men in their various life roles.

> "Therefore confess your sins to each other
> and pray for each other so that you may be
> healed. The prayer of a righteous person is
> powerful and effective" (James 5:16).

One last question to pray about: What does it look like for you to finish well? Certainly for Jesus to quietly affirm you with the words, "Well done." And for your family's love and respect for you to grow so when you go home to be with the Lord, they are able to celebrate your faithful life. You finish well when you daily do God's will. Humble yourself under God's hand so your will aligns with His will. Humility is the channel for God's grace to flow unimpeded into your soul. Prayerfully use these writings to right your relationship with your heavenly Father. Make His Word the last word in your decision making. Time spent with Jesus saves you time!

> "Direct my footsteps according to your word;
> let no sin rule over me" (Psalm 119:133).

Boyd Bailey
Roswell, Georgia

1

Dressed for Success

<hr>

All of you, clothe yourselves with humility toward
one another, for God is opposed to the proud, but
gives grace to the humble. Therefore humble
yourselves under the mighty hand of God, that
He may exalt you at the proper time.

1 Peter 5:5-6 NKJV

I struggle with having a humble heart. When I don't get my way, pride gets in my way. I have a choice—submit to self and become proud, or submit to God and experience humility. Self wants to fight, but the Spirit leads me to walk by faith in peace. It's my choice to live from the point of view of grace or a get-even mindset. Under God's mighty hand, I develop a humble heart. Without Him, I only embolden my pride, but when I put on humility, I dress for spiritual success.

Paul uses the imagery of getting dressed. Each day we choose to put on a prideful attitude or one that esteems others as better than ourselves. When we prioritize another person's needs or desires before our own, we choose to wear the attractive spirit of humility. When we move toward another's perspective and support whatever is important to them, we can delay our own gratification for another day. The choice to be humble facilitates patience and nurtures intimacy.

<hr>

"Humble yourselves before the Lord, and
he will lift you up" (James 4:10).

Who needs your humble response? What problem could be solved by you deferring to another? Perhaps you are in the middle of heated negotiations, and though you believe you are right, you compromise for what's best for the whole. Humility gives in for the sake of the greater good. In your child's activities, you may have occasion to give another family preference even if your son or daughter is more deserving of the opportunity. Generosity is a delicious fruit of humility.

Above all, we trust Almighty God to bring about His best for us in His timing. We may feel hurt or taken advantage of, but we know who is in control. When we give up our right to be right, we can rest in the Lord's righteousness. Our attitude of humility is the result of our will surrendering to God's will. He looks for followers of Christ who die daily to self so He can raise them up for Himself. We demand our way less often and seek His way more consistently. So don't dress up in the apparel of arrogance, but in the gracious garments of humility. God's grace floods into a humble heart.

"Learn from me [Jesus], for I am gentle
and humble in heart, and you will find
rest for your souls" (Matthew 11:29).

Heavenly Father, by Your grace I choose humility over pride. Teach me to rest in You.

Related Readings

1 Samuel 2:7-8; Job 5:11; Matthew 23:12; Acts 20:19; Philippians 2:3

2

Tell the Truth

Jesus answered, "I am the way and the truth and the life."

JOHN 14:6

When he [the devil] lies, he speaks his native language,
for he is a liar and the father of lies.

JOHN 8:44

Truth flows from the One who is the truth—Jesus. Lies flow from the father of lies—the devil. So truth tellers side with the Lord, and liars side with Satan. With whom do we align? We are quick to say Jesus, but in everyday life, if not careful, we can drift into representing the devil. Fear can tempt us to speak untruths, but trust empowers us to speak the truth.

Lying has such a short-term focus. We are afraid we will lose something if we don't lie. We may lose someone's admiration if we don't inflate the truth, but when we are found out to be a liar, we will be humiliated. We may lose money unless we bend the rules, but when indiscretions are exposed over time, we lose more in compromised creditability. Better to lose a little with honesty than a lot with lies.

The devil is an expert in luring us away from the Lord's desires by offering short-term solutions—lies—that lead to long-term destructive consequences. Liars are unable to keep their stories straight, so when confronted they sheepishly say, "I don't remember, or I can't recall what I said." Children who chronically lie seem oblivious; they continue to fib until the pain of not telling the truth causes them to change.

"If we claim to have fellowship with him
and yet walk in the darkness, we lie and
do not live out the truth" (1 John 1:6).

The first lie was presented by the serpent in paradise as he led Eve to believe she could be like God. Some things never change. Every day we are tempted to promote ourselves and pretend we are better than we really are. But Spirit-led living exalts Christ and others, not self. To be honest is to take responsibility for our actions and to avoid blaming others.

"The man said, 'The woman you put here with me—
she gave me some fruit from the tree, and I ate it.'
"Then the LORD God said to the woman,
'What is this you have done?'
"The woman said, 'The serpent deceived
me, and I ate'" (Genesis 3:12-13).

Are you honest with yourself about constant exposure to compromising situations? Are you loose with the truth, or do you speak directly and include all the information? Take responsibility for wrong decisions. Going forward, seek sound advice from friends who will tell you the truth. Be totally honest with them so they can offer the best advice. Begin by coming clean with Christ—He already knows anyway. Then be totally open and real with others.

"Friend deceives friend,
    and no one speaks the truth.
They have taught their tongues to lie;
    they weary themselves with sinning" (Jeremiah 9:5).

What do I need to be honest about with God and myself? Who needs my complete honesty?

Related Readings
Proverbs 12:17; Jeremiah 9:3; Romans 1:25; 1 John 2:21

3

Abundant Forgiveness

*Then Peter came to Jesus and asked, "Lord, how
many times shall I forgive my brother or sister who sins
against me? Up to seven times?" Jesus answered, "I
tell you, not seven times, but seventy-seven times."*

MATTHEW 18:21-22

Sin's offense hurts. There is no doubt about it. Sin wounds indiscriminately. It is no respecter of persons. Sin builds walls. It ravishes relationships and it separates. Sin is a sorry excuse for wrong behavior. Just the sound of the word solicits negative emotion. Sin is deceptive, carnal, and Christ-less. Sin is unfair, sad, and sometimes sadistic.

Sin follows a process of desire, conception, birth, maturity, and death. James describes its diabolical development. "After desire has conceived, it gives birth to sin; and sin, when it is full-grown, gives birth to death" (James 1:15). So sin is not to be taken lightly. Certainly the pain it inflicts cannot be ignored for long. It can kill relationships.

Nonetheless, when someone sins against you, you are to forgive. When their sin assaults your character, you are to forgive them. When their sin berates your work, you are to forgive them. When their sin violates your trust, you are to forgive them. When their sin steals your joy, you are to forgive them.

When someone's sin crushes your dreams, you are to forgive them. When their sin steals from you, you are to forgive them. This level of forgiveness is counterintuitive and countercultural, but it is the way of Christ. Forgiveness is God's game plan. You will lose if you don't forgive. Unforgiveness is torturous to the soul. It is unhealthy for the body and emotions. Unforgiveness fills prescriptions and leaves hollow lives in its wake.

It doesn't matter who is the most right or the most wrong. Forgiveness cuts through the varying degrees of guilt and erases the entire debt. True forgiveness comes from the offended person's heart. It is not a flippant acknowledgment, but a sincere removal of anything that is owed. When the offended one forgives, he or she wipes out the expectation for an apology, a repayment, or change. It is forgiveness, clear and simple. Forgiveness is letting go of the hurt, anger, and shame. When you forgive, you are free. You are free from the shackles of sin. When you forgive, you trust God to judge others in His time. His judgment is just. God can be trusted to handle the consequences of sin's offense.

You continue to forgive others because your heavenly Father continues to forgive you. Without Christ's forgiveness, we are of all men and women most miserable. Jesus does not deal in forgiveness quotas. The forgiveness of the cross was swift, full, and final. Unlock your relational restraints with the key of forgiveness. Write a letter with tear-soaked ink outlining your forgiveness. Call or email someone today and let them know that because you are forgiven, you have forgiven them. Set others free with forgiveness, and you will be set free. There is freedom in Christ. Forgive fast and forgive often.

"Jesus said, 'Father, forgive them, for they do
not know what they are doing'" (Luke 23:34).

Have I accepted Christ's forgiveness? Whom do I need to forgive by God's grace?

Related Readings

Genesis 50:17; Psalm 130:4; Luke 17:3; Ephesians 4:32

4

Out-Give God

⚬⚬⚬

Give away your life; you'll find life given back,
but not merely given back—given back with
bonus and blessing. Giving, not getting, is
the way. Generosity begets generosity.

LUKE 6:38 MSG

It is impossible to out-give the Lord, because He augments any gift given in Jesus's name with His sovereign influence. He can turn a penny into a dime or a dime into a dollar. He can turn a dollar into a hundred dollars or a hundred dollars into a thousand. Eternally motivated gifts grow exponentially.

He can use one life surrendered to Jesus to influence a family. He can use a family under the lordship of Christ to influence a church, a ministry, and a community. He can use a Christ-centered community to influence a state. He can use a state that stands for God's standards to revive a nation. Indeed, He has already used a nation founded on His principles to influence the world. One submitted life is leverage in the Lord's hands.

⚬⚬⚬

"The generous will themselves be blessed,
for they share their food with the poor" (Proverbs 22:9).

Would you be interested in an investment with a 100 percent guaranteed return on investment? In God's economy, this is how He multiplies gifts given for His glory. He receives our ordinary faith offerings as acts of worship and invests them with extraordinary eternal results. Money is not an end in itself, but sometimes it warms a needy heart like nothing else can. Look to give toward ministries that manage His financial resources well.

When you give in Jesus's name, you are giving to Jesus. The Lord is the righteous recipient of your good and generous gifts. Would your motivation to give and the amount you give change if you gave to Jesus in person? Would your heart and posture bow in holy reverence and gratitude? Yes, giving is an act of worship to holy God—not because He needs anything, but because we recognize our need for Him and His reward.

⸺ ◦◦◦ ⸺

> "Whoever is kind to the poor lends to the Lord,
>   and he will reward them for what they
>   have done" (Proverbs 19:17).

Your Master Jesus matches your giving with His resourcefulness and rewards. The Lord has chosen to meet the needs of His people through His people. He even uses unbelievers to care for believers. And the kindness of God through godly people leads those outside the faith to repentance. Your gracious gift, combined with God's grace, is a conduit for people to know Christ. You cannot out-give God. Rather, through your generosity, you work with Him to bring people into the saving knowledge of His Son Jesus.

⸺ ◦◦◦ ⸺

> "Now he who supplies seed to the sower and bread for
> food will also supply and increase your store of seed and
> will enlarge the harvest of your righteousness. You will
> be enriched in every way so that you can be generous
> on every occasion, and through us your generosity will
> result in thanksgiving to God" (2 Corinthians 9:10-11).

Where is the Lord calling me to join Him and aggressively give in the name of Jesus?

Related Readings
Psalm 146:7; Matthew 14:17-21; 2 Corinthians 8:2; Hebrews 6:10

5

Gratitude and Contentment

*Give thanks in all circumstances; for this
is God's will for you in Christ Jesus.*

1 THESSALONIANS 5:18

*I know what it is to be in need, and I know what it is
to have plenty. I have learned the secret of being
content in any and every situation, whether well
fed or hungry, whether living in plenty or in want.*

PHILIPPIANS 4:12

Gratitude and contentment go together like turkey and dressing. They feed each other, and are both fostered by faith. When I remember how God has so richly blessed me, I am overwhelmed by His generosity. For example, I am eternally grateful for His salvation in His Son Jesus. When I think of His gift of grace, I am grateful for its freedom. When I consider His forgiveness, I am grateful for guilt-free living. When I reflect on His love, I am grateful for the ability to love and be loved.

When I think of His holiness, I am grateful that His character can be trusted and is transformational. Stuff is secondary, but the blessings of faith, family, friends, and fitness feed our contentment. We may not have what we want or deserve, but in Christ we have all that is necessary. So be humbly grateful to God, and your contentment will increase.

"The fear of the LORD leads to life;
then one rests content, untouched by trouble"
(Proverbs 19:23).

To be contented is to rest in Christ and trust He is in control. Circumstances, good or bad, are opportunities for Him to show Himself faithful. So once you go to God in gratitude, you can live in contentment, knowing Christ is in control. Contentment is not passive and uninformed; rather, it is engaged and educated. It is not anxious. It replaces worry with work, pity with prayer, hubris with humility, and grumbling with gratitude.

Your peace and stability are the fruit of contentment, which grows in the rich soil of gratitude. Sow seeds of prayer into that soil, and you will reap an abundance. You are able to overcome adversity because the Almighty has gone before you. You are able to keep your desire for riches in check and to give to others because of your gratitude to God and contentment to Christ. Thank God often, and trust Him to cultivate your contentment.

—◦◦◦—

"I can do all things through Christ who strengthens me" (Philippians 4:13 NKJV).

What are some reasons for my gratitude to God, and how can I express my contentment in Christ?

Related Readings
Job 1:21; 2 Corinthians 6:4-10; Ephesians 4:20-24; Colossians 2:6-7

6

Diligence Rules

—◆◇◆—

Diligent hands will rule,
but laziness ends in slave labor.

PROVERBS 12:24

Do you work hard, or do you hardly work? God said to Adam, "Cursed is the ground because of you; through painful toil you will eat food from it all the days of your life...By the sweat of your brow you will eat your food" (Genesis 3:17,19). And He explained to Moses, "Six days you shall labor and do all your work, but the seventh day is a sabbath to the LORD your God. On it you shall not do any work" (Exodus 20:9-10).

Has our culture become accustomed to receiving good things without great effort? Who is entitled to influence without being industrious? Perhaps a dearth of diligence has depressed some people and entire economies. Lazy people want to control others, but honest laborers find new opportunities and advance. Don't despair in your diligence, for you are set for success. Mind your business meticulously, and you'll be much more likely to enjoy it and prosper.

—◆◇◆—

"Now the man Jeroboam was a valiant warrior,
and when Solomon saw that the young man was
industrious, he appointed him over all the forced
labor of the house of Joseph" (1 Kings 11:28 NASB).

Your faithfulness to your work will not go unnoticed. In fact, your industriousness will lead to preferment. Your diligence is a distinctive that separates you from the average or lazy laborer. This level of service brings security. Promotion follows performance that produces the right results the right way. Be an industrious example whom others seek to emulate.

The Lord blesses hands that are hard at work. He smiles when He sees your service exceeds expectations. You go the extra mile to make sure others are cared for as you would like them to care for you. God sees your thoroughness on the job and your integrity in its execution, and He knows you can be trusted with more.

⸺◦⊶◦⸺

"The elders who direct the affairs of the church well are worthy of double honor, especially those whose work is preaching and teaching" (1 Timothy 5:17).

Lord, what task do You want me to diligently complete before beginning another?

Related Readings

1 Kings 12:20; Proverbs 10:4; Romans 12:8; 1 Timothy 4:15

7

A Grace-Made Man

*By the grace of God I am what I am, and his grace to me
was not without effect. No, I worked harder than all of
them—yet not I, but the grace of God that was with me.*

1 CORINTHIANS 15:10

Aself-made man is the antithesis of a grace-made man. A self-made
man becomes desperate for God on occasion, such as whenever
a crisis occurs. A grace-made man is continually desperate for God
because he sees himself as a needy man. A self-made man struggles to
give God the glory for his accomplishments, but the grace-made man
never forgets to give Christ the credit for his success. Grace brings out
the best in humble hearts.

A grace-made man does not work less, but more. Gratitude focuses
grace-based behavior into diligence. A man or woman motivated by
the grace of God works for an audience of One. Their godly ambition has an eternal allegiance that no earthly boss can inspire. We work
hard because God's grace is at work within us. Do your work and life
blend into a divine portrait of grace? If so, you are winning the respect
of those around you.

"For by the grace given me I say to every one of
you: Do not think of yourself more highly than
you ought, but rather think of yourself with sober
judgment, in accordance with the faith God has
distributed to each of you" (Romans 12:3).

We are nothing more than what the Lord makes us by His grace.
We may make money, but unless we lean into the Lord's grace, it is just

another temporal transaction. How can we know we are leaning into the Lord's grace? Our words will be gracious and our attitude humble. We will see people not as a means to make money, but as individuals with hopes, dreams, and fears. We will engage people with kindness, not passive pride.

So work hard with a heavenly agenda. Acknowledge that the larger the Lord's blessing on your life, the greater your need for His grace. Christ increases our capacity to receive His grace as we credit Him for His favor. Amazing grace starts at salvation and becomes a growing marvel as you apply humble faith and thanksgiving. God's grace makes the man; man does not make the man. Your Creator created you and your success. " 'Tis grace hath brought me safe thus far, and grace will lead me home."

"You may say to yourself, 'My power and the strength of my hands have produced this wealth for me.' But remember the LORD your God, for it is he who gives you the ability to produce wealth" (Deuteronomy 8:17-18).

Heavenly Father, teach me to rely more and more on Your generous grace.

Related Readings

1 Samuel 2:7; 2 Corinthians 11:23; Philippians 2:13; Colossians 1:29

8

Motivated by Love

———⁂———

And now these three remain: faith, hope and love.
But the greatest of these is love.

1 Corinthians 13:13

L ove is the highest and best motivation. Like contestants in a beauty
pageant, faith and hope accompany love as the top three finalists,
but love is crowned the winner. It reigns because it brings out the very
best in the lover and the one being loved. Similar to an invisible force
field, love protects us from ourselves and compels us to give ourselves
to others. It generates goodwill and garners trust. Love is the pinnacle
of the Lord's expectations because it points to Christ.

Love is loyal when most are disloyal. Love steps up when some step
away. Love believes the best and doesn't think to assume the worse.
Love looks out for the interests of loved ones above its own needs. Love
always loves—when unloved, when lonely, and when loved. Love loves
the unlovely, the unconcerned, and the underutilized. Love looks for
potential where impatience is disappointed. Love is the Lord's lubri-
cant that causes relationships to run smoothly.

———⁂———

"The only thing that counts is faith expressing
itself through love" (Galatians 5:6).

What is your primary reason for relating to people? Is it to be loved
or to love? Fortunately, when we are free to love without expecting
anything in return, we are fulfilled by love's fruit. Indeed, the glorious
grace of God does not stand still when you run to love someone starved
for compassion. Your gift of love invites the Holy Spirit to spread His

love across the landscape of your heart and soul. Like a fast-spreading plant, love reaches into places we would never expect.

Make sure you are motivated to love by your intimacy with your heavenly Father. Let your communion with Christ inspire you to love others. The more consistent your love relationship with Jesus, the more capacity you have to love. To the extent you are loved well by the Lord, you will love well. The world's noise drowns out the gentle words of Jesus—"I love you." But in your daily quiet time, you hear and feel His presence. God's love motivates you to love with intentionality!

"Dear friends, let us love one another, for love comes from God. Everyone who loves has been born of God and knows God" (1 John 4:7).

Heavenly Father, let Your gracious and generous love motivate me to love.

Related Readings
John 15:12; Romans 5:8,10; 1 Thessalonians 1:3; 3:6; 1 John 4:7-21

Character Is Respected

‹∞∞›

Her husband is respected at the city gate,
where he takes his seat among the elders of the land.

PROVERBS 31:23

Character invites respect and admiration. This comes over time as you establish a track record of consistently doing right. Your character becomes valuable as a creditable community assigns it value. This begins in your home. Do your wife and children (or your roommates) see the same person in private that others see in public? To win the respect of respectable persons, align your private and public character.

The Lord creates His character in us and confers His blessings on it. One of His favorite descriptions of one of His own is a "righteous" man or woman. "The LORD rewards everyone for their righteousness and faithfulness" (1 Samuel 26:23).

Character means something because Christ says it means something. He respects righteousness. Righteous behavior is a barometer of the Lord's blessing. Have you ever observed that other people's character rubs off on you? If you are around a gentle person for long, do you tend to grow in gentleness? If you are honored to see up close the generous deeds of good people, do you become more generous? If praying people regularly lift you and your needs to the Lord, do you find yourself looking for those you can carry to Christ in intercession?

People of character have a profoundly positive effect on you—as you do on others! God created you with an innate desire for authentic respect from those you admire. When you feel respected, you are quick to reciprocate that respect. However, be cautious not to dwell on feeling respected. Instead, extend respect to others. As God develops your character, respect for you will take care of itself. Character is an incubator for respect. You may wonder if righteousness can bring your relationships into alignment. Yes it can! It prepares a road of respect on which relationships can travel smoothly.

—∞∞—

"Righteousness goes before him
     and prepares the way for his steps" (Psalm 85:13).

Respect reaps the rewards of trust and transparency in growing relationships.

Is my character worthy of Christ's respect and the admiration of respectable persons? Do I respect character in others?

Related Readings

Psalms 92:12; 112:6-9; Matthew 1:19; 1 John 3:6-8

Respectable Leaders

*The overseer is to be above reproach, faithful to his wife,
temperate, self-controlled, respectable, hospitable,
able to teach, not given to drunkenness, not violent
but gentle, not quarrelsome, not a lover of money.*

1 TIMOTHY 3:2-3

Respectability invites respect. You may say, "I can't get any respect." If so, on what do you base your expectations? Your charm, your charisma, or your ability to converse well? None of these make you respectable; in fact, they can repel respect and garner disrespect. Your skills and gifts must flow from a strong character in order to garner the admiration of others.

Respect is earned, not demanded. It is sustained by influence, not position. Presidents, preachers, and parents are respected for their position, but if they consistently underperform or lack integrity, respect is lost. Respect is not a right of the irresponsible but a privilege of the dependable. Respectable leaders get right results in the right way.

Respectable leaders also rise to the occasion and do the right things. They persevere and provide stability instead of panicking and creating chaos. They take responsibility by espousing the values of the organization, not by gossiping and blaming others. A depth of character runs deep in their souls, not to be stolen by sin.

Respectable leaders are well thought of because their track record demonstrates trustworthiness, honesty, and follow-through. However, the goal is not for people to like you. They may not like you when you lovingly hold them accountable, but they will respect you. They may not like your discipline, but they will respect your consistency. They may not embrace your beliefs, but if you express them in humility, they will respect you. Ask yourself, "Am I respectable?" If so, you can expect respect.

—————⚬⚬⚬—————

"A sensible person wins admiration,
     but a warped mind is despised" (Proverbs 12:8 NLT).

What area of my character needs growth and transformation in order to elicit respect?

Related Readings
Exodus 18:21; Proverbs 15:27; John 10:12-13; Romans 16:18

Respect the Elderly

⸺◯◯◯⸺

Stand up in the presence of the aged,
show respect for the elderly
and revere your God. I am the LORD.

LEVITICUS 19:32

Years can bring improvement in decision making, perspective, understanding of people, and intimacy with God and those closest to us. The elderly represent a reservoir of wisdom waiting to be tapped. They tell stories of real-life events that challenge, educate, and entertain. Those who love Jesus and are approaching their twilight years have an eternal perspective that is infectious. They see God for who He is.

And yet, though they may have these positive traits, we sometimes hesitate to spend time with the aged, even those who are our own flesh and blood. Why is this so? Yes, some are hard to get along with. Others smell as if they've been trapped indoors (often because they have), and others are high maintenance. This is hard, but it is temporary. Before you know it they will be gone. How many more days do you have with a parent, grandparent, or mentor?

As the sand is rushing toward the bottom of the hourglass, what are some ways you can demonstrate respect toward the elderly? One way is to spend time with them. Consider a regular visit to the nursing home or retirement center. Love on them by showing up with flowers and reading an uplifting portion of Scripture. Listen to their hopes, dreams, and regrets. Capture in your memory the nuggets of wisdom, unique thoughts, and important ideas that remind you of how you want (or don't want) to live your life. Look for snapshots of life that you can emulate and pass along to your children and children's children.

You can also respect your elders by inviting them to visit you rather than you visiting them. Your parents may need to move in with you so you can love them 24/7. Yes, this is a huge commitment. Parenting your parents is more difficult than parenting your children. Their needs are more complicated, and they certainly do not want to be told what to do.

But you love them anyway. You respect them even when they are not respectable. Seize this time. Don't let it slip by in the abyss of busyness. This is your opportunity to teach your kids how to treat you one day. Your respect for the elderly is a reflection of your reverence for God. Love, serve, and respect them as if you were doing the same for Christ.

How can I schedule regular time to learn from and love on the elderly?

Related Readings
Job 32:4-6; Proverbs 16:31; Romans 13:7; 1 Timothy 5:1-2

12

Christ's Calling

He said to them, "Follow Me,
and I will make you fishers of men."
Immediately they left their nets and followed Him.

MATTHEW 4:19-20 NASB

Jesus calls all of His disciples to minister in their homes and in the marketplace. However, He also calls some of His followers to vocational ministry. Many times, this calling comes to ordinary men and women who accomplish extraordinary results. Whom does He call? Christ's call comes to those who have a hungry heart for God.

Like Paul, you might have been smitten suddenly by a revelation of Jesus as Lord. Or perhaps you were like David, who gradually went from caring for sheep to caring for God's people. Wherever Christ calls, His first commands are to love God and to love people. A calling without love is like a car without gasoline. It may be attractive on the outside, but it isn't going anywhere. So love large wherever the Lord has called you.

Furthermore, He has called you to endure hardship. "You have persevered and have endured hardships for my name, and have not grown weary" (Revelation 2:3). Christians are not immune to conflict. In fact, your faith will be challenged at times. So don't seek to shelter your life from adversity. Rather, position yourself in obedience to Christ's calling. Your regular routine of serving Him will help you to see what He has in store.

Make sure you minister first to your wife and children. Don't be like the cobbler who has no shoes for his family. You gain creditability for Christ as you live out your faith with those who know you the best. What does it profit a man if he saves the whole world and loses his family? A calling to family first frees you to evangelize and disciple with God's favor. His calling aligns with His commands, so service for Him is seamless.

Above all, the Lord is looking for those already engaged in His Word, growing in their character, and active in sharing their faith. His calling comes to Christians who desire the Holy Spirit to conform them to the image of Christ. Your humble imitation of Jesus flows from your intimate walk with Him. He calls those whom He can trust. So do not look for your calling. Look for Christ, and He will reveal His calling to you.

─────⁕─────

"I, even I, have spoken;
      yes, I have called him.
   I will bring him,
      and he will succeed in his mission" (Isaiah 48:15).

What is Christ's calling for my life? Am I steadfast in loving the Lord and people?

Related Readings
Acts 9:10; 1 Corinthians 7:17; Hebrews 5:4; Revelation 7:14

Uniquely Gifted

⌐∞⌐

I wish that all of you were as I am.
But each of you has your own gift from God;
one has this gift, another has that.

1 CORINTHIANS 7:7

Our generous heavenly Father gives unique gifts to His children for His glory—gifts of service, encouragement, teaching, mercy, administration, and so on. Regardless of one's role, all gifts are necessary in the body of Christ. One quietly serves as a prayer intercessor behind the scenes while another boldly proclaims truth in front of the faithful. Yes, the Lord specially equips individuals for His good works. God's distinctive gifting is a sign that He values each one of us.

What do you do well? How can you discover your sweet spot of service for your Savior Jesus? One way is to develop your natural abilities and engage in activities that energize you. The Spirit wires you in a way that brings you pleasure when you exercise your gift. For example, a generous giver finds great joy in giving, and evangelists are ecstatic when they share the gospel. An administrator is not content until everyone and everything is in its place.

⌐∞⌐

"We are God's handiwork, created in Christ
Jesus to do good works, which God prepared
in advance for us to do" (Ephesians 2:10).

You may be an analytical thinker who loves crunching numbers, managing data, and interpreting trends. Your gift of linear deduction is critical for business, finance, engineering, and the like. Perhaps you are great with people. People love your company because they sense you know, understand, and care for them. Your ability to network, convene a group, and lead others is valuable for accomplishing a big vision or executing a strategic initiative. Steward well God's unique gift to you.

Seek to marry your passion with your giftedness. For instance, if you love to see someone encouraged, use your gift of writing to convey God's love to their hungry heart. If you love children, use your ability to nurture and train as a conduit for Christ's truth. If you love sports, use your teaching gift to lead athletes in Bible study. If you love travel, use your aptitude for business to help entrepreneurs here and abroad. Be whoever God has uniquely gifted you to be!

———∞∞∞———

"We have different gifts, according to the
grace given to each of us" (Romans 12:6).

Heavenly Father, use my gift from You to bring You glory. Marry Your gift with my passion.

Related Readings
Romans 12:3-8; 1 Corinthians 12; 14:12; Ephesians 4:11-12

14

Good Leaders Follow

*If [your gift] is to encourage, then give encouragement;
if it is giving, then give generously; if it is to lead, do
it diligently; if it is to show mercy, do it cheerfully.*

ROMANS 12:8

Gifted leaders are first and foremost good followers of God. They recognize the gift Giver as their authority, so they do not lord over others. Rather, they submit themselves to the Lord. Because leaders respect Christ, they respect those they lead. Because they love the Lord, they love their team. Because they serve Jesus, they serve those who serve with them. A gifted leader is able to educate a group and influence them toward a common goal. Leaders have followers.

Are you called to lead but held back by feelings of inferiority? If so, find your confidence in Christ. Let Him be your resource for reassurance. Resistance does not mean you are a bad leader. On the contrary, it may be a validation that you are moving in the right direction. Many people struggle when getting on the bandwagon of change—it threatens their security. So stay the course and lead prayerfully, patiently, and lovingly. Trust the Spirit's small voice as it affirms your actions—God is with you.

"Love must be sincere. Hate what is evil; cling
to what is good. Be devoted to one another in
love. Honor one another above yourselves. Never
be lacking in zeal, but keep your spiritual fervor,
serving the Lord. Be joyful in hope, patient in
affliction, faithful in prayer" (Romans 12:9-12).

You know you have the gift of leadership if you can see the big picture and inspire others toward that God-given vision. You understand the sequence of steps required to reach the objectives. You perceive potential problems and make adjustments with wisdom and courage. You motivate the team to embrace transitions as necessary to stay relevant. You create a culture of accountability with real-time updates. No one wants to let anyone down in the execution process.

Your gift of leadership is a weighty responsibility, but you are not alone. Almighty God is your "go to" for humility, holiness, and wisdom. God gives you what you need to accomplish what He wants. Use your leadership role to invest in other emerging leaders. It is harder to grow leaders than it is to lead. Therefore, be intentional and prayerful as you train up faithful men and women who will train others. You steward your leadership best by developing other leaders!

—————— ⌖ ——————

"And David shepherded them with integrity of heart;
with skillful hands he led them" (Psalm 78:72).

Heavenly Father, lead me so that in humility I can lead others in Your ways.

Related Readings
Exodus 32:21; 1 Samuel 18:16; Isaiah 48:21; 1 Corinthians 1:10;
    1 Timothy 6:11-12

Trust Perseveres

∞

For the King trusts in the LORD,
through the unfailing love of the Most High
he will not be shaken.

PSALM 21:7

Trust in God perseveres. It perseveres the higher it goes in responsibilities or the lower it goes in lost opportunities. Whether in the excitement of promotion or the discouragement of demotion, it still trusts God. In fact, the more responsibility we gain, the more we need God. The more capable we seem to be, the more we realize we are incapable without Christ. Power may tempt us to lower our guard in trusting God, but the more responsibility and power we are entrusted with, the more we need to trust the Lord. Kings and presidents need Christ as much as or more than paupers and priests. Trust is not contingent on our felt need. It is contingent on our having a pulse. As long as we have breath, we desperately need the Lord. Self-confidence is an obstacle to our holy confidence in Christ. He sees us through. Trust in Him perseveres.

Trust perseveres because it is buoyant in its belief in the unfailing love of God. The love of God stands secure in the face of suffering. The love of God licks the wounds of a lacerated soul. The love of God provides the grace to forgive and to forget. The love of God continues in the face of ugly odds because of its optimistic hope in Christ. God's love draws us into intimacy with Him. When we know God loves us, we feel safe and secure. When we know God loves us, we feel support and encouragement. The love of God covers our sin of unbelief. It is a buttress for our belief. When we are at our lowest, the love of the Most High lifts us up so we can continue trusting our sympathizing Savior.

He is high and lifted up, so He can lift us up. He looks down on us with compassion. Because He is trustworthy, we trust Him.

No one is higher than Almighty God. He is the Most High. We have the privilege, the opportunity, and the obligation to go right to the top. The Holy Spirit is our guide. By faith we can trust Him to intercede on our behalf. Our faith may be faltering in our confusion, but Christ clarifies. Do not give up because of the complexities of your current situation. Go to the Most High to unravel the mess in which you find yourself. He is the decision maker. He is your Maker. He knows how to guide you through this uncertain process. The Most High has the needed perspective to see you through. By faith, we do not falter. Trust Him to tell you what you need to know. Persevere.

The fruit of trust is perseverance. The high winds of adversity may attempt to uproot your faith, but you will persevere. You will persevere in your marriage even though our culture gives you a pass for divorce. You will persevere in your job even though you have been passed over for someone less qualified. You will persevere as a parent because this may be your time to mature and grow up. You will persevere as a leader because God is not finished spreading your influence. You will persevere as a Christian because you trust God. By God's grace you will not be moved. Allow Him to grow your character. Stand strong. Allow Him to love you through this time of transition. Trust perseveres.

Heavenly Father, I trust You to see me through this hard time at home and at work.

Related Readings
1 Corinthians 13:7; Hebrews 10:36; 11:27; James 1:12; 5:11; Revelation 2:3

We, Not Me

Now you are the body of Christ,
and each one of you is a part of it.

1 Corinthians 12:27

There is a larger context to life than just living for self. A self-focused life is chronically frustrated and unable to reach its full potential. Its demanding demur marginalizes wise counsel and attracts insecure individuals. However, those who pray for what's best for the whole, become whole. Everyone is honored in an environment where individual contributions are valued. "We, not me" is the vocabulary of those who honor each other.

Every disciple is stronger when connected to other Christ followers. Isolation contributes to spiritual impotence, but community gives spiritual life. Encouragement and accountability flow freely in relationships that prioritize what's best for the group. A leader who serves the team will see other team members serve well. A man who serves his family will enjoy a family that serves each other. "We overcomes me" with unselfish service.

"Each of you should use whatever gift you have received to serve others, as faithful stewards of God's grace in its various forms" (1 Peter 4:10).

Our spiritual birth grafted us into Christ's body. We cannot dissociate one of the Lord's appendages any more than we can detach a member of our physical body from the other body parts. So we pray for those around us who know Christ, and we get to know each other. Oh, the joy of being known and knowing others who love Him! Life that is truly life is lived in the margins with those submitted to our Savior Jesus.

Are you motivated first by "He," second by "we," and last by "me"? If so, you are set up for relational fulfillment. The sequence for successful thinking is Him, them, and you. "Me" will try to squeeze in and monopolize relationships, cannibalize conversations, and hijack heaven's agenda. So by God's grace, put to death the "me" monster and replace it with love for the Lord and people. "We, not me" is the motto of mature followers of Jesus.

———— ✺ ————

> "Let no debt remain outstanding, except the continuing debt to love one another, for whoever loves others has fulfilled the law" (Romans 13:8).

Lord, whose needs can I put ahead of mine through my prayers and service?

Related Readings
Romans 12:10-16; 14:13; 15:7; 2 Corinthians 13:11; Galatians 5:13

Image Control

⊂∞⊃

*If someone else thinks they have reasons to put
confidence in the flesh, I have more: circumcised on
the eighth day, of the people of Israel, of the tribe of
Benjamin, a Hebrew of Hebrews; in regard to the law,
a Pharisee; as for zeal, persecuting the church; as for
legalistic righteousness, faultless. But whatever were
gains to me I now consider loss for the sake of Christ.*

PHILIPPIANS 3:4-7

What is image control? It is making sure we appear as we want others to think we really are. Our exterior appearance becomes more important than our interior identity in Christ. We are concerned about, consumed by, or even obsessed with how we look, what we wear, what we drive, what school we attend, where we work, where we live, and so on.

However, image control is exhausting because it never is quite satisfied. Jobs have to be a little more prestigious, cars a little more luxurious, homes a little more opulent, and status a little higher. The curse of image control is subtle because it can be confused with godly ambition, which is good. Here's the difference: The first is about striving for self, and the latter is about dying to self. Godly ambition does its best and trusts the Lord.

Image control suffers from a sense of superiority. It's prompted by pride. Jesus describes a religious leader afflicted by his condescending attitude and lofty self-image. "The Pharisee stood by himself and prayed: 'God, I thank you that I am not like other people—robbers, evildoers, adulterers—or even like this tax collector. I fast twice a week and give a tenth of all I get'" (Luke 18:11-12). Conversely, humility lifts up Jesus, not ourselves.

If we are not halted by humility we become like Narcissus, peering into a prideful pool, loving an image that is a figment of our imagination. Instead, as Spirit-filled followers of Jesus, we see ourselves as precious but peculiar people who are pilgrims just passing through—not encumbered by the weights of worldly expectations, but on our way to heaven. As we journey for Jesus we want our simple life to point others to our Savior.

So who is in control of your image? Have you surrendered your self-image to your Savior Jesus? Let go of the world's shallow sense of worth and embrace your eternal value in the Lord. Almighty God has already set you apart as holy and acceptable to Him in Christ Jesus. He admires and celebrates Your inner beauty more than your outer image.

———ↁ———

"Your beauty should not come from outward
adornment, such as elaborate hairstyles and the
wearing of gold jewelry and fine clothes. Instead,
it should be that of your inner self, the unfading
beauty of a gentle and quiet spirit, which is of
great worth in God's sight" (1 Peter 3:3-4).

How much energy do I exhaust in image control? Do I entrust my image to Christ?

Related Readings
Genesis 37:23-28; Ephesians 1:5-6; Hebrews 11:9-13; 1 Peter 2:9-11

Friendliness Attracts Friends

⚬⚬⚬

A man who has friends must himself be friendly,
But there is a friend who sticks closer than a brother.

PROVERBS 18:24 NKJV

Friendly people are fun to be around. They are upbeat and look for the best in those they meet. Yes, friendliness can come on too strong, but those with relational understanding are sensitive enough to avoid going too far too fast. A friendly person makes you feel at ease and gives you unspoken permission to be yourself. You feel safe sharing your feelings with those who feel what you feel. Friendliness adds emotional energy to the conversation and encouragement to the heart.

Your friendly spirit qualifies you to make friends. Friends want to be around friends who know how to listen and love. Are you the giver in your friendships, or are you the taker? How can you intentionally invest in those the Lord has put in your life? Perhaps you pray by name for your friends' children or even invite their children to visit overnight so the parents can enjoy a 24-hour respite. Friendly people risk making friends and follow with steps to retain friends. Friends care!

⚬⚬⚬

"An unfriendly person pursues
selfish ends" (Proverbs 18:1).

A bond of trust and loyalty grows between two friends who try to out-serve each other. However, if giving goes only one way, over time the giver may grow weary in their solo service. Perhaps your heavenly Father is calling you to fewer but more fulfilling friendships. He may want you to ratchet back your relationships to a manageable number.

Who needs you to go deeper in this season of friendship? Pray for your friend and be emotionally available to enter into his world.

Most importantly, lock arms with the Lord Jesus in your growing friendship with Him. Your maturing friendship with Christ will increase your capacity to love and care for your friends. Friendship with God brings reality to relationships on earth. Ask your friend to bow and pray with you to your mutual friend Jesus. Friends who pray together replace conflict with resolution and anger with joy. Confidants can be closer than blood relatives through the blood of Jesus!

"A friend loves at all times" (Proverbs 17:17).

Heavenly Father, I pray Your Spirit will grow a spirit of friendliness in my heart.

Related Readings

Exodus 33:11; Psalm 109:4; Proverbs 12:26; Acts 19:31; 24:23; 3 John 1

The Great Adventure

—⊶∾⊷—

*By faith Abraham, when called to go to a place he
would later receive as his inheritance, obeyed and went,
even though he did not know where he was going.*

HEBREWS 11:8

We often discern God's will through a series of discoveries. The transitions between these discoveries test the true nature of our faith. We can press forward by faith, or we can analyze the situation until we are paralyzed by uncertainty. Abraham continued toward the unknown because he was certain the Lord was leading him. Great adventure accompanies our obedience to God.

Believers who are bound and determined to obey Christ are not bored. Our love for the Lord compels us to conquer the next challenging circumstance and blaze new trails in prayer. We become soft and satisfied when we stop seeking the next kingdom opportunity. Our Savior Jesus is our guide as we travel in trust.

—⊶∾⊷—

"He guides the humble in what is right
and teaches them his way" (Psalm 25:9).

Are you inspired by your faith adventure, or are you intimidated? Do you anticipate doing the next right thing as you fulfill God's calling on your life, or do you dread whatever is ahead? Christ must come to you in clarity before you venture out for Him in obedience. But once you are sure of the Lord's leading, don't let up until you have arrived at His destination. Go on your great adventure with God and, as if you were on a visit to a new country, enjoy the new sites and people.

The Holy Spirit directs a life that's on the move, not one that's stuck—preoccupied with either pleasure or pain. "A man's heart plans his way, but the LORD directs his steps" (Proverbs 16:9 NKJV). So make prayerful plans, but all the while remain nimble when God's Spirit nudges you. If you fall in love with your plans, you may not notice an adjustment you need to make to follow the Almighty's way.

There is a reward for those who remain true to God's call. It may be simply the satisfaction of knowing you faithfully followed the Lord, but this is all that matters in the end. As a pilgrim passing through this life, launch your next eternal endeavor and experience the righteous ride with Him. Nothing risked may mean nothing lost, but every journey for Jesus holds the promise of great gain. Discover what He wants today, and it will lead to what He wants tomorrow.

"Lead me, LORD, in your righteousness
because of my enemies—
make your way straight before me" (Psalm 5:8).

What great adventure does God have for me? What can I do today to trust and obey?

Related Readings
Proverbs 11:3; Isaiah 48:17; Luke 4:1-2; Galatians 5:16-18

The Pursuit of Pleasure

Whoever loves pleasure will become poor;
whoever loves wine and olive oil will never be rich.

PROVERBS 21:17

The unrestrained pursuit of pleasure leads to poverty. The logical result of a life devoted to pleasure is a man or woman poorly principled, poor with people, poor in soul, and poor in managing God's provision. Pleasure without a greater purpose produces a lame life. However, earthly enjoyments, wed to God's will, open up the windows of heaven. "And he made known to us the mystery of his will according to his good pleasure, which he purposed in Christ" (Ephesians 1:9). His pleasure is good.

Pleasure itself is not evil, but when it competes with our devotion to Christ, it is downright dangerous. Paul said in the last days we will live with this tension.

> "But mark this: There will be terrible times in the last days. People will be lovers of themselves, lovers of money, boastful, proud, abusive, disobedient to their parents, ungrateful, unholy, without love, unforgiving, slanderous, without self-control, brutal, not lovers of the good, treacherous, rash, conceited, lovers of pleasure rather than lovers of God—having a form of godliness but denying its power" (2 Timothy 3:1-5).

Loving God versus loving pleasure. It's not both-and, but either-or. We choose to love Christ or amuse ourselves to death. Luxurious living without the Lord is vain and unfulfilling. When you make pleasure subservient to serving your Savior, you will find fulfillment and peace. Retreat to the beach or mountains to find pleasure in God's creation while enjoying Him and those you love. Enjoyment of life on earth is an outcome of obedience to eternal expectations in heaven.

Find pleasure where your heavenly Father finds pleasure. "His pleasure is not in the strength of the horse, nor his delight in the legs of the warrior; the LORD delights in those who fear him, who put their hope in his unfailing love" (Psalm 147:10-11). We bring Him pleasure by living in humble trust and submission to Him (Matthew 11:25-27). Therefore, take pleasure in Him.

How can I pursue the Lord's pleasures?

Related Readings
Proverbs 10:23; Ephesians 1:5; 1 Timothy 5:6; Hebrews 11:25

Not Too Serious

You who are young, be happy while you are young,
and let your heart give you joy in the days of your youth.
Follow the ways of your heart.

ECCLESIASTES 11:9

Sometimes we take ourselves too seriously. We get caught up in our little world of what we have to do, where we have to go, and who we have to please. Joy is jettisoned from our heart because we are driven by a have-to attitude. Unfortunately for our health and for those who love us, we become consumed by our agenda, our desires, our worries, our ideas, our work, our hobbies, and our needs. Sadly, our unmet expectations become joy killers with no heart.

How do you know whether you are taking yourself too seriously? Suddenly others become the objects of your fury. They don't seem to take things seriously enough. You erroneously think, "If they would just do what I want and work as hard as me, both of our worlds would be much better off!" You act as if the Lord can't get by without you. However, the reverse is true—you can't get by without Him. So shed the world from your shoulders. Consider totally disconnecting from technology on your next vacation. No phone or email. Try it. Lighten up and let the Lord work for you.

"The LORD works righteousness
and justice for all the oppressed" (Psalm 103:6).

What is the solution for taking ourselves too seriously? Humility. A humble heart is free from the motivation of being the main attraction. When we walk in humility, we are content to be behind the scenes and let others receive the attention. Like Jesus and by His Spirit, we empty ourselves of our reputation and expectations, replacing them with His. We let go of our work and let God work. We learn to take ourselves less seriously and the Lord more seriously.

So enjoy the peace and contentment that accompany a non-acrimonious approach to life. Seek harmony, not hostility. Give instead of take. Laugh at yourself and laugh with others over your quirks. Be yourself. Be still. Know God. Joy comes from being with Jesus, so draft behind God instead of striving to get your way. Guard your heart from an overly serious state. Invite Christ's calmness to relax your countenance and restore your smile.

⸺⸺⸺

"Jesus, full of joy through the Holy Spirit, said, 'I praise you, Father, Lord of heaven and earth'" (Luke 10:21).

Heavenly Father, give me the courage to take myself less seriously and You more seriously.

Related Readings
Psalms 19:8; 126:2; Nehemiah 8:10; 1 Thessalonians 1:6; Philemon 7

Spiritual Intimacy

⌖

*The LORD is close to the brokenhearted
and saves those who are crushed in spirit.*

PSALM 34:18

Intimacy with God goes hand in hand with brokenness. In fact, brokenness escorts you into the intimacy you desire with your heavenly Father. It is your date with destiny. A broken and contrite heart makes room for intimacy with the Almighty. Don't despise your broken condition. Rather, delight in the opportunity for intimacy it brings. You have longed to know Jesus in the power of His resurrection and the fellowship of His suffering (Philippians 3:10). These prayers were not in vain. Your brokenness can be the answer to your prayers. It may not be the answer you expected—you may have anticipated a smoother route, a paved road free of bumps or potholes. But the path to a personal and intimate relationship with Christ is not always easy.

Most of the time, intimacy requires difficulty. But of course, at this point of pressure and discomfort, some people disembark the train of intimacy. Talking about an intimate relationship with Christ is much easier than experiencing one through brokenness. To merely talk, however, is to choose convenience rather than commitment. It is like placing a "Do not disturb" sign on the door of your life rather than an invitation that says, "Clean up my room." Brokenness is inviting God to come in and cleanse your life. He stands at the door of our hearts and knocks (Revelation 3:20). When you invite Christ into your broken life, He comes in. You then experience intimacy on His terms, not yours. Only when you surrender in total desperation and total dependency on God do you experience authentic intimacy.

Hardship and brokenness allow you to grow closer to other people as well. A crisis will either drive you further from people or closer to them. God's best for you includes making your relationships stronger during a season of brokenness. But brokenness is not a one-time phenomenon. It is an ongoing part of the committed Christian's life. It's not as if you swallow this hard pill one time and are set for a lifetime of intimacy with God. Once God has marked you with brokenness, you are positioned for Him to build on this firm foundation. He will still use brief moments of brokenness throughout your life. These regular occurrences are like bricks, cemented together by His grace, to build His home in your heart.

Your brokenness is meant for your betterment. Indeed, you are much better for having endured a defining moment of brokenness. These moments deserve your embrace rather than your rejection. If you fight brokenness, you delay God's best and circumvent intimacy with Christ. Focus your energies on changing yourself, not your circumstances. Christ will handle the circumstances while you adjust your attitude.

A life of brokenness is an invitation to intimacy. His closeness and salvation are worth the price. Don't short-circuit this process. Instead, rely on Him and get to know Him at this deeper level of intimacy. You are much better when you are broken because brokenness leads to intimacy with God.

Heavenly Father, break my heart over what breaks Your heart. Draw me into deeper intimacy with You.

Related Readings
Psalms 34:20; 51:17; Isaiah 61:1; Hebrews 7:18-9; 10:22; James 4:8

Emotional Intimacy

⸺ ◦⸰⸙⸰◦ ⸺

That is why a man leaves his father and mother
and is united to his wife,
and they become one flesh.

GENESIS 2:24

Growing relationships require regular investments of emotional energy. Only humans have the capacity for emotional engagement—a level of feeling and understanding that machines or animals can never attain. Created in God's image, we are able to engage in intimate encounters. Emotions are meant to move people toward the eternal.

Marriage partners especially require growing emotional intelligence to thrive and not merely survive. The Lord has created an emotional vacuum in husbands and wives that only their spouse can fill. It is folly to ignore this very real need for the sake of careers or children. Using these things as substitutes will only stunt emotional maturity. To be one flesh is to forge an alliance and an allegiance of minds, wills, and emotions.

⸺ ◦⸰⸙⸰◦ ⸺

"[Love] always protects, always trusts, always
hopes, always perseveres" (1 Corinthians 13:7).

Jesus joined you and your wife together in holy matrimony. Are you growing in oneness? To share your passion is only to take one step. You have a lifetime to explore the world of feelings in your marriage bond. Make emotional investments in your marriage as you begin to understand each other's needs. Are attention, security, and communication her top three needs? God gives you wisdom so that you can really come to know your wife.

You probably take time to consider your financial investments and save for the future. In the same way, take time to make wise emotional investments in your marriage. Emotional deposits today will yield unity and oneness tomorrow. Otherwise, you will grow old apart rather than together.

By faith, we become one with Christ. Then, with love, patience, and understanding, we become one with each other. Your oneness in marriage illustrates your faith in Christ.

"We ought always to thank God for you, brothers and sisters, and rightly so, because your faith is growing more and more, and the love you have for one another is increasing" (2 Thessalonians 1:3).

Lord, what do I need to know about my wife so that she feels loved and accepted by me?

Related Readings
Galatians 5:13; Hebrews 12:3,15; 1 Peter 2:2; 2 Peter 3:18

Physical Intimacy

‒‒‒‒‒‒‒‒‒‒‒‒‒‒∞‒‒‒‒‒‒‒‒‒‒‒‒‒‒

The marriage bed must be a place of mutuality—
the husband seeking to satisfy his wife, the wife
seeking to satisfy her husband. Marriage is not a
place to "stand up for your rights." Marriage is a
decision to serve the other, whether in bed or out.

1 CORINTHIANS 7:3-4 MSG

Our marital duty is neither to demand sex nor to endure sex, but to see it as an expression of love and respect. You have the unique privilege to connect with your wife at spiritual, emotional, and physical levels. Physical intimacy is a privilege reserved for marriage. Done well, it takes time and planning. Yes, there are those spontaneous intimate rendezvous, but we need to be students of our wife's needs and desires. Connecting emotionally and communicating throughout the day often leads to physical intimacy at night.

The richest and most fulfilling physical intimacy flows out of emotional intimacy. When a husband and wife connect emotionally, they are better primed to connect physically. Indeed, physical intimacy is more than a transaction—it is a relational process that often finds its highest expression in the event of two becoming one. Women who deny their husbands for an unreasonable time can unwittingly signal disinterest and disrespect. Men who rush past the emotional needs of their wives ignore their need for security, attention, and respect.

‒‒‒‒‒‒‒‒‒‒∞‒‒‒‒‒‒‒‒‒‒

"How beautiful you are, my darling!
     Oh, how beautiful! Your eyes are doves."
"How handsome you are, my beloved!
     Oh, how charming! And our bed is verdant"
     (Song of Solomon 1:15-16).

Reserve the marriage bed as a sanctuary for sleep and an enclave for physical intimacy. Avoid other activities in the bedroom—this is not the place for television, food, computers, sleeping kids, and dogs. Create a haven for physical intimacy, and you will experience greater oneness. Throughout the day, be intentional about creating emotional chemistry with notes, phone calls, caring words, empathetic listening, gifts, and kind acts of service.

As followers of Jesus, and because of your spiritual synergy and emotional engagement, you and your wife have the opportunity for the most fulfilling physical intimacy. Ask the Lord for creative ways to love your lover as she loves to be loved. Your marriage relationship illustrates the relationship between Christ (the groom) and His church (the bride). Indeed, physical affection flows from spiritual and emotional intimacy. So be prayerfully intentional and watch your relationship go from good to great for God's glory.

***

"Like an apple tree among the trees of the forest
 is my beloved among the young men.
I delight to sit in his shade,
 and his fruit is sweet to my taste.
Let him lead me to the banquet hall,
 and let his banner over me be love"
 (Song of Songs 2:3-4).

Heavenly Father, give me the grace and wisdom to connect with my wife spiritually, emotionally, and physically.

Related Readings
Genesis 4:1; 25:21; Song of Songs 2:14; 4:16; 1 Peter 3:7

God's Purpose

∞

I cry out to God Most High,
to God who fulfills his purpose to me.

PSALM 57:2 ESV

God in His providence has a personal purpose for each of His people. Our gracious God grants us wisdom into His ways. He wants us to experience His eternal aims for His glory. Paul affirmed the providential fulfillment of God's purpose. "I always pray with joy…being confident of this, that he who began a good work in you will carry it on to completion until the day of Christ Jesus" (Philippians 1:4,6). God began fulfilling His purpose for us when we placed our faith in Jesus. This was our contract with Christ that placed the responsibility of fulfilling His purpose at the feet of our heavenly Father. Our Lord will finish everything He has begun since we first believed in Him. Whatever the Lord takes in hand, He will accomplish. So we trust the Almighty with the fulfillment of His purpose for our lives.

Our role is to pray so we can know His ways and cooperate with Him. Prayer positions us to live out heaven's purpose for our life. We cry out to the Most High because nothing and no one is any higher. He is at the top. He is the divine decision maker. He is our Maker. There is no one else we can ask to show us the purpose for our lives—only the Lord Jesus Christ. Faith is not dumb. We pray because we believe there is a better way than we can know through our own very limited wisdom. We can get by with the wisdom of the world, but we can thrive with the wisdom of Almighty God. We cry out to Christ because He has adopted us. We define our purpose by our heavenly Father's purpose for us. Prayer pulls out His purpose front and center.

Prayer is proof of our trust in God. When we send our prayers to heaven, God sends help from heaven. Unless we pray, our trust will fail us. Trust becomes trivial unless persistent prayer backs it up. Prayer brings trust into the reality of God's promises and purpose for our life. Prayer is potent because it aligns us with the purposes of Almighty God. Once we understand our own personal purpose, we can rest assured God will follow through and fulfill it on our behalf.

Put pen to paper and prayerfully define your God-given purpose. Use this definition as a filter for decision making. This becomes your accountability to God and others to say no. Lean into the Lord, asking Him to lead you in His purpose for your life. Once you have established His purpose for you, leverage that for others. Use the strength of your position to help others discover their God-given purpose. Have them list their gifts, skills, passions, and experiences. Pray with them about how God wants to maximize their effectiveness for Christ. Assure them that their heavenly Father will fulfill His purpose for them, as He did with His own Son at just the right time (Galatians 4:4-5 NASB).

Be patient as God implements His purpose for your life. Remember that you are living His purpose now. No season of life is insignificant in the Lord's eyes. Don't wish away where you are today. By faith, you can be sure that Christ is currently fulfilling your purpose. Make sure your goals are God-given and then trust Him with their fulfillment. Be prayerful and patient as God performs His purpose in you!

Heavenly Father, help me to prayerfully align my purpose with Yours. Make my ways Your ways.

Related Readings
Psalm 138:8; Isaiah 55:9; Romans 1:10; 1 Thessalonians 4:3; 5:18

Mission Accomplished

—— ∞ ——

*For a long time now—to this very day—you have
not deserted your fellow Israelites but carried
out the mission the LORD your God gave you.*

JOSHUA 22:3

What is your personal mission? Your professional mission? Are they clearly defined, and do they align? Your mission is your purpose in life; it is why you get up in the morning. Is yours compelling and Christ-centered? Your mission flows from your heart, mind, and soul. It is who God made you to be and what He wants you to do. Are you on your mission from God? A purposeful life produces lasting results blessed by the Lord.

Your mission keeps you honest and accountable. It is what God uses to measure the effectiveness of your life. He has created you for a specific purpose with a specific plan. You can rest assured that your mission involves loving Him and loving others, as these are His two greatest commandments. "'Love the Lord your God with all your heart and with all your soul and with all your strength and with all your mind'; and, 'Love your neighbor as yourself'" (Luke 10:27). Love lingers long on behalf of the Lord.

A clear sense of your mission can be a time-saving filter for decision making. It gives you permission to say no to many things and yes to a few things. Your mission is your friend, your motivator, and your protector. Embrace it and let it empower you. Then live your life intentionally rather than drifting and missing God's best.

How can you discover and live out God's mission for your life and work? Start with God. How has He gifted you? What are your passions, and what do you do well? Will the mission you are considering be pleasing and acceptable to God and to those who care about you the most? What are your roles in life? You may be a son, a daughter, a brother, a sister, a parent, a friend, a leader, a husband, or a wife. Consider the influence of your life's roles and weave those into your purpose.

Your personal mission and professional mission should be aligned. For example, if your personal mission is to be family friendly and your professional responsibilities require you to travel extensively, you may need to reevaluate. If your career is currently demanding an inordinate amount of time, make sure your wife and children understand this is temporary so they can support your efforts.

Use your mission to monitor your activities—are they a reflection of who you really are? Intentionally establish your identity according to God's definition. Consider what He would have you do at this stage of life, for your mission can evolve over time. Write it down, update it whenever necessary, and keep it in front of you. Then one day, you can say, "Mission accomplished," just as Jesus did: "I have brought you glory on earth by completing the work you gave me to do" (John 17:4).

Note: My personal mission is to glorify God by being a faithful husband, available father, loyal friend, and loving leader. My professional mission is to love the Lord and love people through devotional writing that applies the unchanging truth of God's Word to a changing world.

What is God's purpose for my personal and professional life? Are they aligned? Am I "on purpose" for God?

Related Readings

Exodus 9:16; Psalm 57:2 (esv); 2 Thessalonians 1:11; Revelation 17:17

27

Monetize Your Mission

⸺⸺⸺⸺⸺

*The master commended the dishonest manager
because he had acted shrewdly. For the people of this
world are more shrewd in dealing with their own kind
than are the people of the light. I tell you, use worldly
wealth to gain friends for yourselves, so that when it is
gone, you will be welcomed into eternal dwellings.*

LUKE 16:8-9

Creating an economic structure around passion and purpose can be a prayerful and godly goal. It could mean converting informal, free advice into a formalized fee for coaching, consulting, or counseling. It may mean engaging a hobby of painting, writing, or singing and moving it into the market as a valued product. God gives us gifts and skills so we can earn a living. There are times to give away time and expertise, and there are times to monetize our mission.

Making money is not our motivation, but it is a by-product of determining what wakes us up in the morning and making that valuable for others. Why waste our lives just working for a paycheck when we could be creatively channeling our energies and experiences into an economic endeavor? Christ commends His servants who innovate new ways to make friends and influence people. Indeed, we are called to be creative for Christ's sake.

⸺⸺⸺⸺⸺

"'I was afraid and went out and hid your gold in the ground. See, here is what belongs to you.'

"His master replied, 'You wicked, lazy servant! So you knew that I harvest where I have not sown and gather where I have not scattered seed? Well then,

you should have put my money on deposit with
the bankers, so that when I returned I would have
received it back with interest'" (Matthew 25:25-27).

You are wise to work in your area of expertise, but avoid ruts that lead to complacency. Pray about how the Lord wants you to steward the relationships, opportunities, and gifts He has given you. Perhaps a small group of friends will pray with you and even invest some seed money to help you monetize God's mission for your life. Truly, compared to eternity, life is a blink of an eye, so don't hesitate on His direction.

Servants of Jesus need not be paralyzed by fear. Instead, by faith, follow the Holy Spirit's promptings in your heart. Don't talk yourself out of following a promising new course for your career simply because it's unconventional. The world will watch with admiration a shrewd servant of the Lord who, with an eye on eternity, invests in people. Your life is attractive when you live out your mission with passion and productivity. Trust God to give you the wisdom to make a living by following His call.

———— ∞ ————

"The one who calls you is faithful, and he
will do it" (1 Thessalonians 5:24).

Lord, how can I monetize my mission for the sake of Your kingdom?

Related Readings
Proverbs 22:29; 2 Corinthians 5:1; Ephesians 2:10; 1 Timothy 6:17-19

28

Business as Mission

⸺ ∾∾∾ ⸺

Paul went to see [Priscilla and Aquila], and because
he was a tentmaker as they were, he stayed and
worked with them. Every Sabbath he reasoned in the
synagogue, trying to persuade Jews and Greeks.

ACTS 18:2-4

Business is an opportunity to be an excellent example of a Jesus follower. Use your professional platform to perform good deeds and exhibit integrity in business interactions. Your kingdom mission and your role in business can work together as you model actions that speak louder than words. When the quality of your work exceeds industry standards, people begin to ask why.

A company that acknowledges Christ as the owner is positioned for God's favor. Do the values of your company mirror the heart of Jesus? Do you and your coworkers embrace honesty, humility, and hard work as everyday virtues to live out? Are team members quick to serve, eager to find solutions, and careful to give positive feedback? If our work culture reflects the character of Christ, we will attract team members who can take the company to the next level. Great people are not motivated by money alone, but by a mission much greater than themselves. Greatness comes to a company with a greater purpose.

⸺ ∾∾∾ ⸺

"You yourselves are our letter, written on our
hearts, known and read by everyone. You show
that you are a letter from Christ, the result of our
ministry, written not with ink but with the Spirit
of the living God, not on tablets of stone but on
tablets of human hearts" (2 Corinthians 3:2-3).

Is your real mission just to make money, or is it to transform lives? Does your team go the second mile for customers, or are clients merely means to a financial end? An enterprise that glorifies God with outstanding service and superior products will produce fruit that remains. Become better, and you will become bigger for the right reasons. Your work done well is a testament to God's grace, faithfulness, and favor.

Furthermore, a leader who submits to the Lord does not lord it over other team members. A humble leader leads and manages from a heart of appreciation and accountability, not as an intimidating, autocratic ruler. Even supervisors or employees who don't believe in Jesus can embrace His ethics. When we create a culture friendly to faith, we grow a team of people who have faith in each other.

Therefore, intentionally integrate scriptural principles into your life and work. Use your business or ministry to make life better for people and people better for life. Be bold to tastefully and professionally pray for people. Give team members time off to invest in their marriages and travel on mission trips. Grow leaders who will educate, train, and inspire their teams. Dedicate your company to Christ, and He will determine your steps for success.

———∞∞———

"In their hearts humans plan their course,
     but the Lord establishes their steps" (Proverbs 16:9).

Heavenly Father, I dedicate this company to You for Your purposes.

Related Readings
Exodus 32:16; Jeremiah 31:33; 1 Thessalonians 2:9;
   2 Thessalonians 3:8

29

Spiritual Leadership

———— ⁂ ————

*If serving the LORD seems undesirable to you, then choose
for yourselves this day whom you will serve, whether the
gods your forefathers served beyond the Euphrates, or
the gods of the Amorites, in whose land you are living.
But as for me and my household, we will serve the LORD.*

JOSHUA 24:15

What does it mean to be the spiritual leader of my home? Do I
have to reach a certain level of spiritual maturity before I qual-
ify? What if my wife is more spiritual than I am? Shouldn't she be the
spiritual leader?

Spiritual leadership is determined by position, not knowledge. God
places a man in the role of spiritual leader to lead his wife and children
in faith. Our wives and children may know more of the Bible, but the
Lord still holds us responsible for their spiritual well-being. So as husbands and fathers, we have to ask ourselves, "What am I doing to lead
my family spiritually?" This assignment from Almighty God forces us
into faith-based behavior. We want to model daily time in Bible reading and prayer. Spiritual leaders show the way in knowing God.

———— ⁂ ————

"The jailer brought them into his house and
set a meal before them; he was filled with joy
because he had come to believe in God—he
and his whole household" (Acts 16:34).

Spiritual leadership does not require a graduate degree in theology,
but it does require some degree of planning and preparation. A spiritual leader creates a prayerful plan of intentional action that exposes his

family to faith-building opportunities. Spend time looking for houses of worship that meet the needs of your wife and children, much as you would seek out a home or school that meets their needs. Spiritual leadership seeks out a church.

———✎———

"Let us go to his dwelling place;
       let us worship at his footstool" (Psalm 132:7).

Men who make it a big deal to lead their family spiritually make the most difference at home and in the community. Your investment in family Bible study, your example of faith under fire, and your Christlike character are living testaments to the truth of God. Talk about the Lord when you linger in traffic with your children, pray with them when they are fearful and upset, hold your wife's hand and listen to her heart, sign up for the next marriage retreat, and serve others unselfishly. You can't control the culture, but you and your house can serve the Lord. Spiritual leaders lead their family to love God.

———✎———

"The husband is the head of the wife as Christ
is the head of the church, his body, of which
he is the Savior. Now as the church submits
to Christ, so also wives should submit to their
husbands in everything" (Ephesians 5:23-24).

How can I take responsibility to lead my family spiritually? How can I leave a legacy of serving the Lord?

Related Readings
2 Samuel 12:20; Psalm 100:4; Acts 18:7; 2 Timothy 1:16

30

Eternally Motivated

---

*[Moses] regarded disgrace for the sake of Christ
as of greater value than the treasures of Egypt,
because he was looking ahead to his reward.*

HEBREWS 11:26

Eternal rewards are based on a disciple's effort on earth. Believers who ignore their spiritual opportunities and obligations will miss out on their heavenly Father's affirmation and remuneration. But sober saints who take seriously their Savior's expectations will enter into the joy of their Master. Christ rewards our obedience to Him.

Rewards in heaven are meant to provide godly motivation. Yes, our first response is to serve Jesus out of love and our overflowing gratitude for His goodness and grace. And it is wise to fear the Lord and allow our holy awe of the Almighty to be foundational for our life of faith and works. But there is an end in mind. Jesus wants His children to be devoted and compelled by anticipating His generous gifts.

"The Son of Man is going to come in his Father's glory
with his angels, and then he will reward each person
according to what they have done" (Matthew 16:27).

It is a process of renewing your mind with an eternal decision-making filter that facilitates biblical thinking and doing. Ask the Lord how He wants you to invest your life in others. How does God want you to use your experience, your assets, your time, your money, and your influence for His purposes? In other words, how can you make eternal investments on earth that bear fruit for God's glory?

What you do does not get you to heaven—this comes only by faith in Christ and God's amazing grace. But what you do after becoming a follower of Jesus does determine the quality of your eternal experience. The persecuted and martyred in this life have a great reward waiting in the next life. Those who initiate resources and influence on behalf of the poor and needy bring great satisfaction to Jesus, which He expresses in bountiful blessings. Indeed, He rewards all those who diligently seek Him by faith.

"Without faith it is impossible to please God,
because anyone who comes to him must
believe that he exists and that he rewards those
who earnestly seek him" (Hebrews 11:6).

Love God, and your reward will be great. Be a faithful witness who plants or waters the gospel of Jesus Christ, and you will be rewarded by spending forever with eternally grateful souls. Send your investments ahead to heaven by aggressively giving them away on earth. Reject rewards from the culture so you are positioned to receive Christ's rewards. Remain faithful to God's call and look forward to His reward.

"Look, I am coming soon! My reward is with
me, and I will give to each person according to
what they have done" (Revelation 22:12).

How can I live my life in a way that honors the Lord and looks forward to His rewards?

Related Readings
Amos 6:1-7; Isaiah 54:2; 2 Peter 1:3; Revelation 2:7-10

31

Divided Against Itself

❧

Jesus knew their thoughts and said to them, "Every kingdom divided against itself will be ruined, and every city or household divided against itself will not stand."

MATTHEW 12:25

Humility unites; pride divides. Patience pauses; anger accelerates. When families, cities, or nations are divided, an implosion takes place, and their significance is reduced to rubble. Ongoing battles in the home build walls, ruining communication and intimacy, teamwork and trust, peace and contentment. Indeed, the devil uses division as one of his primary weapons because it leads to worry and fear. If he can divide husbands and wives, he has conquered them. Division defeats marital maturity and replaces it with childish tirades.

When husbands and wives think the other has become the enemy, the enemy has won. When people are divided, they are deceived into thinking they cannot work together, so they fight it out. The entire process is irrational and irresponsible.

Anger drives division. There is an obsession to have one's way regardless of the shattered outcome. Things are done just to spite the other. Patience is thrown to the wind and replaced with accusations and insults. Division is the fruit of pride. There is no room for compromise, much less death to self. It drives couples to unreasonable demands and proud pontifications. Division creates losers and lasting regrets. It's a road that leads to a downward spiral of ineffective living.

Therefore, unite around humility. Humility relates from a position of brokenness. It appeals to the common sense of Christ and the wisdom of God. Mutual submission to your Savior Jesus becomes the starting point of discussion. Divorce is off the table, and no position comes between the parties. This is how division is defeated. There is a determination by everyone involved to depend on God and godly counselors for instruction and accountability. Emotional hostage-taking is prohibited, and manipulative moves are unacceptable. Instead, the fruit of the Spirit (Galatians 5:22) is the baseline for discussions. Unity is fostered in respectful and responsible discussions. This is the place where patient and cool heads prevail.

Lastly, identify the true enemies—pride, fear, selfishness, and the demons of hell. Make a frontal assault of faith on the adversary instead of backstabbing each other with betrayal. Unity flourishes in a foray into forgiveness. "Forgive first and discuss second" is a good rule of thumb. Unity requires thinking the best of each other. Past failures are not held over the other as a hammer of guilt, and current hurts are not glibly dismissed. Unity makes room for healing to take place.

People who pray together unite over time. Unity is a beautiful outcome for couples who pray together. As your heads hit the pillow each night, pray for one another before you slip into sleep. Let nighttime prayers calm you before you doze off and dream. United, your marriage and ministry will stand; divided, it will fall. Therefore, unite around God and His Word. In Christ, you will stand (Philippians 1:27). Stand strong with your Savior. He forgives. He saves. He unifies.

Heavenly Father, grow in me a humble heart that unites, not a prideful heart that divides.

Related Readings
Genesis 2:24; Romans 6:5; 12:5; 1 Corinthians 1:10; 6:17;
    Galatians 5:22

32

Built to Last

⁘

Woe to him who builds his palace by unrighteousness,
his upper rooms by injustice,
making his countrymen work for nothing,
not paying them for their labor.

JEREMIAH 22:13

Anything worth doing is worth doing well. If you are building a family, frame it well. Furnish it with faith, love, hope, and the fear of God. If you are building a business or ministry, grow it relationally and systematically. Pour a foundation of honesty, trust, and excellent work. If you are building a life, develop it with discipline, forgiveness, humility, grace, service, and obedience to God. Spend your time building people, processes, projects, and enterprises that are sustainable and eternal. Focus on endeavors that contribute to and facilitate faith-based initiatives. Build people who will improve on your accomplishments. Above all else, dedicate your building to God.

You are positioned as a leader, so lead well. You have the stewardship to mentor others, so pour yourself into those who will become mentors themselves. Build spiritual disciplines into faithful followers of Christ. Do not neglect developing disciples. Disciples of Jesus need a firm foundation of faith.

It is imperative to model for them mastery of the Master's words. Let the Word of God flow freely from you. Speak it and live it on behalf of your Savior. You build lives that last when you ground them in the Bible. The legacy you leave is predicated on the people in whom you invest.

Therefore, keep your children "top of mind." Make them your number one building project. Begin to tell them about Jesus when they are still tiny. As they grow, instill the principles of Scripture into their hearts and minds. Relate to them stories of God's faithfulness in your life through the years. Confess how your heavenly Father forgave you at your points of failure. This authentic home environment grows small children into giants of the faith. Build into your children now, and they will leave a legacy of faith later. Build for generations to come.

In addition, build your ministry or business into one that lasts, assuming it is the Lord's will for it to last. A business or a ministry that is built to last is carefully constructed with the bricks of vision, mission, and values. They are embedded in the foundation of the enterprise. Strategy, objectives, goals, and metrics all flow from the same source. Where there is vision, there is a compelling cause that motivates everyone. Where there is mission, there is clarity of purpose. Where there are values, there are agreed-upon behaviors that define the culture.

If your vision is too small, only little people will venture forth. If your vision is so massive that it becomes unrealistic, no one will take you seriously. However, if your vision is prayerfully aligned with God's will, He will accomplish great things through you and others. Cast a God-sized vision that will last beyond your lifetime. Keep your team focused on mission-critical initiatives. These are building blocks for the business. Wise leaders learn to run with what works and dismiss what doesn't. Tell stories that illustrate your mission. This keeps everyone focused on the reality of why they show up every day. Don't get so busy that you forget to review God's building plans. What He builds lasts as long as He wills.

Heavenly Father, give me the patience and perseverance to build on Your firm foundation.

Related Readings
Nehemiah 3:1; Psalm 48:13; 1 Corinthians 3:10-12; Ephesians 2:20

33

Teach Children Wisdom

———— ❧ ————

Pains as of a woman in childbirth come to him,
but he is a child without wisdom;
when the time arrives,
he doesn't have the sense to come out of the womb.

HOSEA 13:13

Children need to be taught wisdom. Yes, sometimes it's hard for them to grasp its meaning because of their age and stage in life. Wisdom comes through understanding and applying God's Word to life experience. Many individuals are limited in their perspective of both, so shared wisdom guides them away from unwise decision making. Wisdom is one of the most wonderful gifts you can give your child, so make it inviting and practical.

Tell stories of individuals who made wise decisions and the positive effects that followed. Then contrast these uplifting illustrations with stories of those who chose an unwise path and suffered harm as a result. Stories stir the heart and illuminate the mind. We owe it to our offspring to engage them in conversations about real-life people. Otherwise, they remain oblivious, living in a bubble of unrealistic expectations.

They grow in wisdom by spreading their wings and making decisions while they still live under your roof. Start them out young by helping them make money decisions. Show them the pattern of "share, save, and spend" from your own financial management. Lead them to do the same. Watch them smile as they experience the joy of generosity. Be proud as their discipline and patience grow. They will be able to save for something they want and purchase their prize with cash. Be an example of smart spending, and you may become a recipient of its fruit as your child learns how to be a savvy shopper. Financial wisdom is a practical gift. Use its principles to train your child.

Good judgment in choosing friends is another facet of teaching your child the ways of wisdom. Make sure children understand the propensity to become like the people they hang out with. Teach them to choose friends whose faith is growing and robust, friends who lift up instead of those who pull down. Help your kids to avoid flirting with friendships that dilute growth with God. Discuss why they need to avoid friendships that become a wedge between child and parent. Wisdom does not settle for the shallow acceptance of just any friend. Wisdom sets a high standard for friendship. Challenge your children to pray for friends who complement their faith, who move them closer to their heavenly Father. Wise friends rub off on your children in wise ways.

Talk regularly with your children about the wisdom of God. He gives wisdom. Read with them from the Bible and discuss the meanings of particular verses. Make the discussion of Scripture a part of your everyday life. Take your Bible to church. Underline the phrases that leap from the page into your heart and mind. Then discuss their application to your life over lunch. Invite your child to hold you accountable to the truth God is teaching you. You cannot improve on the wisdom of the Lord. God's wisdom will follow them the rest of their lives. It will be with them when you are absent. You can be at peace when you have a child who is wise in the ways of God.

You are wise when your goal is to grow a wise child. Wise children become wise adults.

Heavenly Father, teach me wisdom so I can train and teach my children Your wisdom.

Related Readings
Job 12:13; Proverbs 2:6; 13:20; Ephesians 6:4; James 1:5

34

Leadership Void

The idols speak deceitfully, diviners see visions that lie;
they tell dreams that are false, they give comfort in vain.
Therefore the people wander like sheep
oppressed for lack of a shepherd.

ZECHARIAH **10:2**

People wander aimlessly without leadership. They would much rather be led by loving leaders who listen to the Lord and who listen to them. Look for leaders like Solomon, who asked the Lord to teach him how to lead: "Give me wisdom and knowledge, that I may lead this people, for who is able to govern this great people of yours?" (2 Chronicles 1:10). This is God's design, for He has wired people to resist wandering and to want leadership. You are a follower of Jesus Christ and a follower of those He has placed in authority over you.

If someone in a position of leadership does not lead, there is doubt and confusion. People wander around, disconnected and disinterested, because they are unsure of where to turn. But eventually, some ambitious soul will fill the empty shoes of leadership even if he or she is unable to lead effectively. A silent coup takes place when responsible leaders abdicate their leadership. When someone without a calling to lead and with an untested character backs into leadership by default, the result can be worse than no leadership at all.

People can easily lose perspective and settle for less than the best. Hungry for a leader, they can use poor judgment. This happened to the people who begged Samuel for a king but later regretted their request (1 Samuel 8:4-21). Therefore, do not settle for anything less than God's choice. Be prayerful and patient; God will send His called leader in His timing. It is better to have an open position of leadership than to fill it with the wrong person. Extracting a lackluster leader can drain resources and emotions. Wait and work toward God's best. Whether you are searching for a pastor, CEO, headmaster, administrative assistant, COO, or wife, continue to trust God for His choice. Don't just fill a slot for the sake of expedience. Make vitally sure their chemistry, character, and competence align with your culture.

If you are already in a position of leadership, "lead, follow, or get out of the way." People expect you to lead, and they are confused if you don't. What are you waiting for? You will not lead perfectly, but press on. Faithful followers are not looking for perfect leaders. They are praying for honest leaders whose passion is fueled by the Holy Spirit.

Leaders who love God and people will never lack a following. Let go of your fear of leading, release control, and have faith that God has placed you in this position of leadership. He equips those He calls to carry out His assignment. You may lead here for just a season, so lead with abandon on behalf of the Almighty. Seek the Lord as the leader of your life, family, work, and ministry. Follow hard after God so you can effectively lead people. Ask Him for wisdom and stay focused on the mission. Get your marching orders from on high and then execute them down below. Effective leaders love to lead, and their Holy Spirit–infused energy engages others in shared goals. Perhaps the people are looking to you for leadership. Therefore, on behalf of your Lord and by His grace, follow Him and lead them.

Heavenly Father, lead me by Your Spirit to love and lead according to Your will.

Related Readings
Psalm 78:72; Proverbs 11:14; Matthew 20:26; Luke 6:31; John 3:30;
     Philippians 2:3

35

The "D" Word

*Therefore what God has joined
together, let no one separate.*

MARK 10:9

Divorce is not an option for committed followers of Christ; it is omitted from their vocabulary. Yes, in their human frailty, they may want an out. People don't enjoy being uncomfortable or inconvenienced, but God uses marital challenges to purge His people. Relational reconciliation in marriage is the proving ground for all other relationships. Marriage mandates focused fidelity to God and faith in Him, for it is not a relationship of convenience, but of conviction. You cannot give up on your wife, except in the case of adultery. And even in unfaithfulness, her repentance and your forgiveness can heal the severed trust and intimacy.

Marriage is a reflection of your Master. Whatever God does is not to be taken lightly, and the Lord is in the marriage-making business. He joins a man and a woman together in marriage as a mirror of their relationship with Him. It is final and forever.

There is no need to run and hide when you let down your spouse. When the bubble of marital bliss bursts, be kind, patient, and forgiving. Begin by allowing Christ to cleanse your heart because left on its own, the heart becomes selfish, proud, immature, and demanding (Matthew 15:19-20). Therefore, put self into a deep sleep and hypnotize it with heaven's expectations. Jesus came into your life so you could be a servant to all, especially your wife. He gives you peace so you can be a justice of the peace in your home under the power of the Holy Spirit. A Christ-centered marriage creates peace and quiet, so submit to the Lord together and experience Him who produces a peace that passes all understanding (Philippians 4:7-9).

God's marriage design prevents destruction by divorce. It creates environments where you encourage and build up each other. Children feel the safest in families where divorce is not an option. The Lord hates divorce (Malachi 2:16 NASB) because He knows it results in a lifetime of disappointment and disillusionment. One way to decrease divorce is to exalt marriage. Make marriage mean something by seeing it as a mandate from your Master. Accept marriage as a privilege and a responsibility. Marriage is a not a man's free pass for sex or a woman's gateway for security.

Marriage is a divine appointment for a lifetime; it is not a temporary assignment until things get difficult. To marry is to enlist to serve your wife on behalf of your Savior. Marriage is designed to draw you closer to God in dependence and trust; it is a facilitator of faith. God uses marriage to reflect His glory and His unconditional love and forgiveness.

If divorce is your secret trump card when things get rough, you are destined to ruin your marriage with a self-fulfilling strategy. Therefore, agree together to get rid of divorce talk forever and become broken before the Lord. See your marriage as sealed by the Holy Spirit, never to be separated by man. Your marriage is not a mistake, so persevere in hope. You were joined together in marriage by Jesus and for Jesus. And your marriage is not to be destroyed by man's decree of divorce.

Heavenly Father, just as You covenant with me in our relationship, I covenant with my wife in marriage.

Related Readings
Psalm 105:8-11; Matthew 19:3-9; Philippians 4:7-9; Hebrews 6:17-18

36

Motivated by Money

⚬⚬⚬

Jesus entered the temple courts and began driving out
those who were buying and selling there. He overturned
the tables of the money changers and the benches
of those selling doves, and would not allow anyone
to carry merchandise through the temple courts.

MARK 11:15-16

A motivation to be rich is not helpful. In fact, it can make you downright miserable. It frustrates you and those around you because money-motivated people are never content. They have an insatiable desire for the next deal or the next opportunity to make more. An all-consuming desire for money leads you to compromise common sense and character. Ironically, your family suffers the most even though your desire is for them to enjoy the benefits money may produce. Some money-motivated individuals stoop so low as to use the Lord to line their pockets. Religion and church become means to create cash. This angers God, for He is moved by righteous indignation when His bride is prostituted for worldly purposes. The church is a conduit for Christ, not a clearinghouse for economic gain. It is a house of prayer (Isaiah 56:7).

God is greatly grieved when money becomes the driving force of any institution or individual. A church bound up in debt is destined for ineffectiveness. If the bride of Christ is preoccupied with paying the bills, the mission will be watered down or even ignored. Money-driven ministries miss the opportunity to trust God and wait on Him to provide in ways that exceed human capability. Businesses that are driven exclusively by bottom-line performance create an unhealthy company culture. People are willing to earn less at a company that has a much bigger vision than just making money. There is so much more to life and work than money (Matthew 6:25).

Money motivation is the antithesis of mission motivation. The latter has a greater purpose in mind. The focus is on excellent work accompanied by eternal expectations. The mission drives you to do more because a transcendent spark ignites your soul. When the mission creates a culture of care and collaboration, money becomes a result, not the reason to exist.

The mission gives you permission to say no. Enterprises and individuals are defined more by what they say no to than by what they say yes to. A well-focused team makes a habit of defending the mission. Disciplined decision making characterizes mission-driven people and organizations. Paul said, "One thing I do: Forgetting what is behind and straining toward what is ahead, I press on toward the goal" (Philippians 3:13-14).

Mission is the master of money, so focus on the mission of your Master Jesus, and you will be much more productive in the long run. Mission motivation keeps you trustworthy, effective, and blessed by God.

Heavenly Father, my love and affection are for You and not for money.

Related Readings
Psalm 49:17; Luke 16:10-14; 1 Timothy 6:6-10

37

Overcome by Fear

*Then all the people of the region of the Gerasenes
asked Jesus to leave them, because they were
overcome with fear. So he got into the boat and left.*

LUKE 8:37

Fear drives out faith, disconnecting us from Jesus. Jesus is a gentleman, so He does not tarry where He is not trusted. He does not remain where He is not wanted, and He does not negotiate to be needed. Faith is exhausted in the face of overwhelming fear. This is especially true when your chronic fear relates to money. Money, more than anything, can make you myopic, enticing you to focus on your need rather than your faith in God. You get so consumed by the current crisis that you forget your anchor in Almighty God. Your desire for money, or your fear of not having enough, may be killing you. However, a focus on money is a symptom of something else beneath the surface of your fears. Money is not the answer. Jesus is the dependable security you desire.

Do not dismiss prayer and patience just because you feel out of control. This is where you are tempted to behave like an atheist. You say the right things—you believe in God, He is in control, and you trust Him—but your behavior betrays your beliefs. You act like an unbeliever when your actions marginalize your Master. When the bottom falls out, let your faith in the Lord be your mainstay. "Be still, and know that I am God" (Psalm 46:10). This is when you need Him the most, so be wise and ask gentle Jesus to remain with you when all hell breaks loose.

Satan loves to see you alone. He wants you to battle him in your own strength. He wins when Jesus is run off and fear drives your irrational actions. Fear keeps you looking over your shoulder in doubt.

And all the while, your Savior is right beside you, waiting to be your calming force. Take the time to tarry in trust with the One who is totally trustworthy. Do not drive Him away in denial. Rise up from under your load of care and come to Christ. Look to Him for perspective and patience. Don't panic. Exercise your overwhelming fear by faith. Place it on the shelf of self-denial and surrender to your Savior.

Now is your opportunity to stand firmly and courageously in Christ. Do not run Him off, for He will stay only where He is wanted. Talk is easy, but your walk with Him matters most. He desires an authentic and teachable heart. He can create this in you by faith. So let these uncertain times embolden you and strengthen your beliefs. Go deeper with Jesus during desperate days. He is a gentleman waiting for your invitation to stay. When fear attacks, be comforted by Christ's confidence and warm embrace.

∞

"The LORD is my light and my salvation—
whom shall I fear?" (Psalm 27:1).

Be real with those around you. Some of them have traveled this road before you, so learn from them. Trust them as a resource, for fear is flattened by the faith of friends. Trust them and trust God. Fear flees in the face of faithfulness, so escort the fear of failure out the door. Above all else, be strengthened by faith's reassurance and not weakened by the fear of financial loss.

Heavenly Father, teach me to fear nothing but You.

Related Readings
Genesis 15:1; Psalm 56:4-11; Daniel 10:12-19; Hebrews 11:23; 13:6

38

Saving the Best for Last

*Everyone brings out the choice wine first and then
the cheaper wine after the guests have had too much
to drink; but you have saved the best till now.*

JOHN 2:10

Jesus sometimes saves the best for last. He delights in delivering the unexpected to the unsuspecting. He waits until there is opportunity to show up where the needs are rampant but the solutions are few. Then He meets the need unconventionally and boldly. Many times, this is His method because Christ is counterintuitive. He wants others to ask why.

Why did Jesus save the best for last? One reason the Lord saves the best for last is to honor the recipients. Those who persevere deserve the best. For example, in relationships, the fruit of long-term commitment produces the best experiences. Trust, contentment, and fulfillment all earn their right in relationships that resolve to remain true.

God blesses those who wait. "Wait for the LORD and keep His way, and He will exalt you to inherit the land" (Psalm 37:34 NASB). You experience the best God has to offer when you save yourself for marriage. Sex within the bond of marriage exceeds exponentially the counterfeit—premarital, hormonal-driven sex. When you act on impulse, you risk disease and a lifetime of disrespect and regret. Patience brings out the best, for trust in God fosters hope that there must be something better to look forward to in the future. It protects you from impatient impulses that can instantly implode.

Waiting for the best is difficult at times because it means depending on others to accomplish the goal. The outcome is out of your direct control. You have to trust that others can execute the project better than you can by yourself. Your sphere of influence will shrink if you try to do everything yourself. You will be limited by your time, energy, and intellect. Your capacity is a drop in the bucket compared to the resources of an aligned team. You need each other's gifts and skills (Romans 12:4-5). Your best brings out the best in others. So be the best at what you do, and expect others to do their very best. Excellence attracts excellence, just as mediocrity attracts mediocrity. Be the best that you can be and see to it that others do the same.

Trust Jesus to bring out His best in people and circumstances under your influence. Let go and let the Lord run with the opportunity. He may surprise you with joy. The best is yet to come if you look to the Lord for His best outcomes. Your humble request of God will result in much more than you thought you were capable of, for Christ has no capacity issues. He is looking for those whom He can trust with His best. He wants those whose faithfulness to Him far exceeds their earthly ambitions. Do whatever He says and watch Him carry out His very best, because obedience leads to His best.

Believe the best is yet to come and don't settle for less. Believe the best in others. Trust God for the very best. Expect the best and be your best. Pray and ask God for His best. Be patient, wait on Him, and remind yourself often that He saves the best for last.

Heavenly Father, grow my faith and patience to wait on Your very best.

Related Readings
Psalm 130:5-6; Proverbs 20:22; Isaiah 26:8; Lamentations 3:24-26; Jude 21

39

Stubborn Pride

*I will break down your stubborn pride and
make the sky above you like iron and the
ground beneath you like bronze.*

LEVITICUS **26:19**

Stubborn pride creates hardened hearts. It is shortsighted and insecure in its aggressive attempts to control. Stubborn pride acts
as if it has everything together and doesn't need help from anyone—
even God. People with this stiff attitude can be frustrating when you
are attempting to work out conflicting issues. The demands of stubborn pride are unreasonable, and its perspective is skewed toward itself.
Stubborn pride resists change and misses out on improvement for the
sake of the project, the team, or the family. Everyone has to be careful
of stubborn pride sneaking into his beliefs and behaviors.

Stubborn pride rejects authentic relational engagement, which
requires confession and forgiveness. Stubborn pride will dig itself into
a deeper hole of distant living rather than risk being found out. But discerning people recognize the charade people play when they are unable
to admit their faults. Stubborn pride is seductive, but it melts under
the heat of humility.

God has a way of wresting control away from stubborn pride. He
will not stand by and allow stubborn pride to suffocate His servants.
His passion is to break its spell and bring His children into relational
reality. When you reject stubborn pride and live in humility, you fight
fair together. You truly listen to the perspective of your wife or coworker
without reacting defensively or judging too quickly. You are willing to
change for the greater good and to please your Savior.

The Lord loves us too much to stand by while we struggle under
the influence of stubborn pride. Like wild stallions with plenty of

willpower and energy, we need to be broken and trained. Almighty God is our Master and trainer. He uses whatever means necessary to get our attention. His Holy Spirit is assigned to break our will and align our spirit with His. God is the One trying to get our attention. We may be mad at others, but our case is against Christ.

The Spirit's conviction causes us to cringe at stubborn pride's relational poison. Christ's brokenness leads us to release control and trust Him. He breaks us of our need to control. He breaks us to be bold for Him. He breaks us and molds us into reasonable people who honor other people's views. Do not negotiate with stubborn pride—break it under the hammer of humility and replace it with love, respect, and forgiveness.

"The eyes of the arrogant man will be humbled
    and the pride of men brought low;
  the LORD alone will be exalted in that day" (Isaiah 2:11).

Heavenly Father, I humble myself under Your mighty hand and ask You to drive pride from my heart.

Related Readings
Exodus 10:3; Proverbs 11:2; 16:18; 18:12; James 4:10; 1 Peter 5:5

40

Pride Forgets

⸺⸺⸺ ∞ ⸺⸺⸺

*Your heart will become proud and you will
forget the LORD your God, who brought you
out of Egypt, out of the land of slavery.*

DEUTERONOMY 8:14

A prideful man forgets where he came from. He seems to forget his humble beginnings and dependence on others. He may get promoted, but he forgets who contributed to his success or furthered his career. He gives too much credit to himself and gives too little credit to others.

A prideful man can forget his family. Sometimes he gets so busy in work or play that he doesn't include the ones who provide the platform for his performance. A prideful man takes his family for granted and ignores their needs. He ignores other people's feelings and is insensitive, obnoxious, and wrapped up in himself.

A prideful man is not afraid to crush someone's spirit on his own way to success. He forgets others, but a humble man includes others. A prideful man takes all the credit, but a humble man shares the credit. A prideful man discourages, but a humble man encourages. A prideful man pontificates, but a humble man prays. A prideful man talks too much, but a humble man listens liberally. A prideful man blames, but a humble man takes responsibility. A prideful man is oblivious to good manners and courteous conduct. He is all about himself with little or no regard for the needs of others.

Above all else, a prideful man forgets God. He may talk about God but only to rubber-stamp his plans. He subtly uses God to carry out his agenda and forgets to see God for who He is. Almighty God is high and lifted up. He is holy, and He expects us to love, fear, and obey. A prideful man forgets that God governs the universe and all its inhabitants.

God is engaged with you up to the smallest of details—He knows where you are and where you need to go. He wants you to remember His pristine track record of trustworthiness. His past provision is a predictor of His future faithfulness. A prideful man forgets this; he has amnesia when it comes to the things of the Almighty. A prideful man may say he believes in God, but he acts like an agnostic. He is too busy to create margin for his Master.

At all costs, allow Christ to keep your pride in its place. It can be conquered only with humble dependence on God and obedience to His commands.

A humble man leaves no room for pride and bows before God in prayer. He remembers God's faithful deliverance from darkness into light. He remembers God's salvation from sin and self to grace and service. He remembers to love God and people first and his own needs second. He has tremendous recall for good because God is his leader. He remembers how generous God is, and he is generous in return. He understands and remembers what's important to the Lord and then invests his energies toward God's initiatives. A humble man remembers to thank others and to pray for them. He is grateful and appeals to heaven on behalf of people.

"Seek the Lord, all you humble of the land,
    you who do what he commands.
Seek righteousness, seek humility" (Zephaniah 2:3).

Heavenly Father, keep me humble and teachable. Remind me of Your love and faithfulness.

Related Readings
Proverbs 16:5; 27:2; 29:23; Jeremiah 9:23-24; Galatians 6:3; James 4:6

41

Face Time

*I have much to write to you, but I do not want to use
paper and ink. Instead, I hope to visit you and talk with
you face to face, so that our joy may be complete.*

2 John 12

Some things are best communicated face-to-face. A proposal of marriage, a job interview, a mentor relationship, family time, explaining an issue, showing appreciation...these work best one-on-one. Fear would force us away from direct engagement with people. We sometimes avoid human contact because of overwhelming insecurity, fear of rejection, or busyness. The season of face time with family quickly evaporates. Kids are off with friends, attending college, and then married.

So schedule time daily, weekly, monthly, and yearly with those you love. Invest time and money in face time with your son, your daughter, your wife, your parents, and your friends. Face time is when you see the fear in their eyes and extend the encouragement to continue. Face time allows your smile to shine a ray of hope across a discouraged heart. Face time is your opportunity to discuss those hard issues and to be sure the sincerity of your love shines through. So show up and love on others in person.

Most important, we need face time with our heavenly Father. By faith, the eyes of our soul need to gaze at God. If we chronically miss coming alongside Christ, we burn out in our own strength. We desperately need face time, by faith, with Jesus. We need His affirmation and love, we need His instruction and correction, we need His warm embrace, and we need His discernment and wisdom.

He can give us all of these anytime. Our Savior is spontaneous for our sake. Christ is on call for His children, but we still need structured time with Him. It is imperative that we instill in our lives the discipline of daily face time in prayer and God's Word. Regular face time with God in Scripture transforms our minds with truth and saves us from the lies of lazy living.

You can tell when someone has been with Jesus. He has peace that brings calm, patience that extends a second chance, and boldness based on wisdom. He has love that forgives, service that is relentless, faith that is strong, and a hope that perseveres. People who have regular face time with Jesus are unique and winsome.

So linger with the Lord face-to-face. Invest time in your relationship with the Almighty. Keep an eye on eternity. Then create face time with family, friends, and those you lead and serve. Trust and intimacy grow when you look into each other's eyes. Take the time to discuss hard issues in person. Provide constructive and courageous feedback. Forging face time means you care. Faithfulness in face time leads to robust relationships. Enjoy being with Jesus and your friends.

"The LORD would speak to Moses face to face,
as one speaks to a friend" (Exodus 33:11).

Heavenly Father, I trust You to make up for any time I spend face-to-face with You or with those who love me the most.

Related Readings
Numbers 12:8; Deuteronomy 5:4; 34:10; Isaiah 26:17; Jude 24

42

Continue Encouragement

⟨≈⟩

*Therefore encourage one another and build
each other up, just as in fact you are doing.*

1 THESSALONIANS 5:11

People die a thousand deaths of discouragement as their daily lives sap courage from their hearts. We all need courage, primarily from the resurrected life of Christ. He is our hope. He is our Savior. He is our Lord. He is our life. Because Christ is in you, you may be able to share the dose of courage a friend needs to make it through another day. Don't underestimate your ability to dispense courage. Your kind word and warm smile are encouraging. So are your generosity, your presence, your listening ear, your investment of time, and your wisdom. Your encouragement builds up others.

When Satan tears people down, you build them up. His goal is the demolition of faith, hope, and love. Your God-given mandate is the building up of faith, hope, and love. Where Satan discourages, you encourage. Like an opponent in a chess match, he is trying to deceive others into thinking they are trapped with no way out. He plays for a checkmate of discouragement, but you have courage and hope in King Jesus. He already has the devil checked, and there's no possibility of a stalemate. So use eternal encouragement to deliver others from the devil's delusions. Take courage from God so you can give courage to others. Lead others to this same fountain of eternal encouragement so they can drink from it when no other encouragers are around.

Courage is to the soul what food is to the body. It is satisfying at the time but exhausts itself quickly, so dine at the table of God's encouragement regularly. His Word is sumptuous, satisfying, and encouraging. Dispense His Word to others in doses of daily encouragement. Human words are hollow compared to the meaty words of Scripture. The

Bible is a reality check. It's full of bold encouragement—when you are immersed in the Holy Scriptures, you are covered with encouragement.

It is not possible to consistently feed on the Bible and not be encouraged! Believe His Word, and you *will* be encouraged. His promises are true—He has forgiven you, He has accepted you, He loves you, He walks with you, and He desires you. This is encouraging! Be encouraged so that you can encourage others.

Encouraging others is also encouraging. When you see a person breathe a sigh of relief, you are encouraged. When you see them do the wise thing, you are encouraged. You train a child in the way he should go. Then he lives for God, and you are eternally encouraged. Give courage, and you will receive courage. Choose the high road of encouragement over the low road of discouragement. Anyone can discourage, so don't be just anyone. Be a Barnabas ("son of encouragement")—God will be pleased, and you and many others will be encouraged.

"Rise up; this matter is in your hands. We will support
you, so take courage and do it" (Ezra 10:4).

Heavenly Father, give me courage to continue encouraging others to trust You.

Related Readings
Psalm 10:17; Acts 4:36; Ephesians 4:29; 1 Thessalonians 4:18

43

Exceed Expectations

*Confident of your obedience, I write to you,
knowing that you will do even more than I ask.*

Philemon 21

Exceed expectations because God has done the same for you. He has done everything He said He would do and more. There is nothing halfway about God. He does things right and then throws in some extra, overwhelming us with His grace. Therefore, when God or others ask something of you, go for it with gusto. Exceed expectations. Make it a goal to bring more value to a relationship than you receive.

If someone asks for prayer, pray right then and there. Make it a habit to pray regularly for those in need, especially those who request prayer. Exceed expectations in your prayer for others.

Exceed expectations in your work. Don't just get by with the minimum requirements, but let your work bring glory to God. What better way to make Christianity attractive than to work with excellence?

When you exceed expectations, you open the door for others to inquire about your motivation—serving and pleasing the Lord Jesus. Exceeded expectations may facilitate advancement in your career. People want to work with and for someone who goes the second mile. They want to reward and hang out with someone who exceeds expectations. When we exceed expectations, we know that at the very least, the One we serve will be satisfied.

Exceed expectations with your attitude. A positive, can-do attitude goes a long way toward making relational deposits. There are a lot of things we cannot control, but our attitude is one thing we can. Go over the top with an attitude of gratitude and generosity. Be exceedingly grateful!

Your marriage provides plenty of chances for you to serve beyond what is expected. Make it a goal to out-serve your spouse. Marriage is an opportunity to give respect. No one complains of too much love and respect in their marriage. You can't give your wife too much respect or love. Look for creative ways to love and respect her beyond her expectations.

Exceeded expectations in the home make for harmony and contentment. The home is all about others, not you. Yes, there are times you feel the need to be spoiled, but first seek to spoil and serve others. You receive blessings and encouragement beyond measure when you serve in ways that exceed others' expectations. It's not a zero-sum game—you don't keep score of who has done the most for the other lately. Rather, you die to your own expectations so you can exceed your family's expectations.

You can exceed what God expects of you. Model this for others. Why just get by with God? A prayer of salvation is just the beginning of your belief and your lifetime love affair with the Lord. He has a treasure trove of adventure waiting for those who will take him at His word and dare to exceed His expectations. So if God asks for 10 percent giving, exceed His minimum requirement. If He asks for one day of Sabbath, give Him daily mini Sabbaths. If He asks for your heart, give Him your life. Go more than one mile for another by giving others what they don't deserve. Exceed expectation for heaven's sake.

Heavenly Father, by Your grace I hope to exceed others' expectations for Your glory.

Related Readings
Luke 17:10; Romans 15:17; Galatians 6:14; Philippians 3:3

44

Attention to Detail

———— ∞ ————

*Are not five sparrows sold for two pennies? Yet
not one of them is forgotten by God. Indeed, the
very hairs of your head are all numbered. Don't be
afraid; you are worth more than many sparrows.*

LUKE 12:6-7

Attention to detail means you care. When you show keen interest in something or someone, you demonstrate that you value them. This is what your heavenly Father does. No concern misses His interest. God knows every bird. From the smallest hummingbird to the largest condor, He cares for each one.

Yet a bird's worth cannot compare with your incredible value. That would be like comparing a sliver of glass to a radiant diamond, a bicycle to a Mercedes, a tiny nest to a huge mansion. It is laughable to consider any similarity in value. God values you as we would the jewelry, the automobile, and the home. Your worth outstrips anything else in all His creation. You are the pinnacle of His portfolio.

You are His most valued asset, and He knows and understands the details of your life. Of course, He is more intimately involved with you than you are. This is reassuring. You may feel trapped in a maze of uncertainty. Life could not be more confusing. Your marriage is in chaos. Your career has hit a dead end. Your finances are at a new low. Moving forward feels like walking through a marsh of molasses. Life is not fun right now, but the One whose eye is on the sparrow has set His heart on you.

His care is beyond your comprehension. He is relentless and reassuring in His compassion. Let Him into the details of your life. He already knows, and He has your best interest in mind. Your heavenly

Father knows what is best for you. No need to fear—God is as near as prayer. His attention to detail invites you to trust and lean on Him.

If details are important to God, they should be important to us. But details are not always easy to manage. They can become cumbersome and cranky, a rat's nest of responsibility. But you can surround yourself with people who are passionate about things that you are not. People's passion points flush out important details. It may be time for you to trust others with some critical details screaming for your attention. They will probably manage them better than you do anyway. Even though you are still accountable for the results, delegate the responsibility. This will free you up to give broader vision and leadership.

You cannot cover all the details—only God has that capacity. You will go to an early grave if you stay on this obsessive trajectory. A supportive assistant is invaluable, so start there. Keep the big picture in focus, and give close attention only to the smaller details that you alone can manage. Otherwise, you will be average at best in your execution. Most of all, trust God and others with the shepherding of details. But as you trust, provide friendly follow-up. You can do for others what God is doing for you, for He gives loving attention to the details surrounding your life. Replace fear with faith and hope in Him.

"We wait in hope for the LORD;
    he is our help and our shield.
In him our hearts rejoice,
    for we trust in his holy name" (Psalm 33:20-21).

Heavenly Father, thank You for Your compassionate care for every detail of my life.

Related Readings

1 Kings 6:38; 1 Chronicles 28:19; Psalm 139:13; Matthew 5:18; 2 Peter 1:21

45

Battle Fatigue

⸺ ◦◦◦ ⸺

*Once again there was a battle between the Philistines
and Israel. David went down with his men to fight
against the Philistines, and he became exhausted.*

2 SAMUEL 21:15

When we're exhausted, we're excellent candidates for encouragement. We cannot continue alone in our exhaustion. Our body and soul cry out for care. If we ignore exhaustion's warning signals, we will probably fail. Our health may fail, our judgment may fail, our faculties may fail, our faith may fail. Exhaustion increases the probability of failure. It is imperative that we recognize our exhaustion and receive help from others. We have to trust that they will keep our best interests in mind. We are unwise if we think we can do everything. This overwhelmed state compromises the quality of our work. Things that we would usually take care of slip through the cracks. In our exhaustion, excellence exits our work and life.

Our character becomes fragile under the weight of exhaustion. As with a clove of garlic in a press, the sweet juices of God's grace are squeezed out of us, and we are left dry. Our patience becomes thin, and we lash out at those who deserve much better from us. Things that don't bother us when we are rested soon become stressful. Meaningless arguments fill our minds, leaving no room for pleasant thoughts. Exhaustion pushes us to the edge. We are more likely to listen to foolish talk and make unwise engagements.

In our exhaustion, we are drawn to any understanding ear and any warm body. We tend to relax our conservative convictions. So especially when you are tired, make sure you confide in your spouse, not someone else. Intimacy is meant for marriage, so leverage exhaustion for a deeper relationship with your wife.

Exhaustion is also God's way of getting your attention. You cannot continue to run ahead of the Lord. He wants much more than surface acknowledgment on Sunday. Exhaustion can engage you with the eternal. You are reminded, in your weakened state, that God is your rock. He is your fortress, your deliverer, your shield, your stronghold, and your salvation. Because God is your refuge, you can rest in Him. You do not have to strive in your own strength. You can be infused with the Almighty's eternal energy and everlasting love. Your heavenly Father wants to love you wholeheartedly and unconditionally in your exhaustion.

So let go and let Him. Let go of unrealistic expectations that wear you down. Let go of your way of doing things. Let go of your timetable. Let go of relationships that are wearing you out. Engage in activities and relationships that energize you. Yes, you need to be available, but rest in God and leave the rest to Him. Your gracious heavenly Father is the answer to your battle fatigue. Invite the Holy Spirit to fill you up by faith, and allow God's grace to flush out your fears.

"Yes, my soul, find rest in God;
     my hope comes from him" (Psalm 62:5).

Heavenly Father, strengthen me by Your Spirit to persevere under pressure.

Related Readings

Numbers 10:9; 1 Samuel 17:47; Psalm 140:7; Hosea 1:7; James 4:1-10

46

Process Disappointment

Cast your cares on the LORD and he will sustain you;
he will never let the righteous be shaken.

PSALM 55:22

Process your disappointment, or you will remain in its downward spiral. Let your disappointment drive you toward God and not away from Him. If disappointment is not processed, it harms our heart. It builds up like emotional plaque and blocks the flow of the Holy Spirit from Almighty God to us. The Spirit is quenched, and we are left to function in our own strength. This is a lonely place.

Unprocessed disappointment leads to angry reactions. Whether it leaks out gradually or explodes unexpectedly, it is ugly. It causes others to ask, "Where did that come from? Is he okay?" Disappointed people become dreadful to be around. They are unhappy with themselves and everyone who surrounds them.

Disappointment is here to stay, but we can learn to process it quickly and move beyond its influence. Disappointment may come from a broken promise or an unmet expectation. You may find disappointment when you look in your checkbook or flip through your calendar. You may face it after you step on the scale or make an unwise purchase or commitment. Most disappointments have to do with people. They let you down, they don't act right, they don't give you the respect you deserve, or they don't seem to care.

If disappointment is a fact of life, how can we process it in a healthy manner? How can disappointment work to our advantage instead of our disadvantage? To process disappointment properly, begin by seeking God's perspective. Align with His view on the matter, asking questions like these: What does God want me to learn from this disappointing situation? How do I need to change? How can I be a blessing to others in the middle of my extreme disappointment? How can I shift my focus away from my disappointment and toward His faithfulness? These questions and others like them help us process disappointment in a way that makes us more dependent on God and less dependent on circumstances. He understands our disappointment and wants to meet us in the middle of our hurt. But He meets with us to move us beyond our disappointment. Connecting with our Savior provides true satisfaction.

So don't remain stuck in your disappointment. You can stop assigning blame and start laying claim to the Lord. Christ overcame His own extreme disappointment when He cried out, "My God, My God, why have you forsaken me?" (Mark 15:34). He cares for you and gave His life on the cross for you. Your Savior Jesus will sustain you in and through your disappointment.

Make regular appointments with your heavenly Father to process your disappointment. Flood your soul with His grace and forgiveness. Pray for those who have let you down, and see them as God sees them—as people who desperately need His care. The way you process disappointment testifies of your trust in Jesus. Therefore, cast your cares on Christ and receive God's care so you can care for the disappointed. Process your disappointment by the grace of God, for His hope overcomes disappointment.

"Hope does not disappoint, because the love of God
has been poured out within our hearts through the
Holy Spirit who was given to us" (Romans 5:5 NASB).

Heavenly Father, in my disappointment and my uncertainty of what to do, I lean into You. I need Your grace to forgive and remain faithful.

Related Readings

Psalm 22:5; Isaiah 49:23; 58:11; Jeremiah 2:36; Luke 3:13;
    Hebrews 13:5

47

Temporary Setbacks

They went immediately to the Jews in Jerusalem and compelled them by force to stop. Thus the work on the house of God in Jerusalem came to a standstill.

EZRA 4:23-24

Don't give up. You may be facing a temporary setback, but God's purposes will not be thwarted. It may seem as if life is on hold and everything has come to a standstill. You have worked so hard to get to this point, and now the opportunity seems to have vanished. Hold it with an open hand, as it may have disappeared. If so, God has something better.

This is not the time to get mad, but glad. What God initiates, He accomplishes. He hasn't forgotten about you or your circumstances. He is on top of the situation. This is a temporary setback. Now is a good time for you to catch your breath and reflect on the great things He has done so far. You have been running hard, so pause and prepare for the next stage of personal and professional growth. You do not need to venture into opportunities for which your character is not ready. The last thing you want is to move forward without the depth of wisdom, patience, relationships, and operational skills needed to complete the project. Your adversaries' motive is to crush your project, but God is taking what was meant for evil and using it for good.

Others use unfair criticism as a cheap way to distract you. Ignore their immature insults. Do not lower yourself to their level of behavior. Otherwise, you may never get out. If you become defensive, you'll just spin your wheels and probably get stuck. Focus on God, not your detractors. He has led you this far, and He will lead you through to completion. If everything were easy, we might take God's blessings for granted or forgo gratitude to God.

The Lord knows what is best. He knows how to align the hearts of everyone involved in the project. Sometimes there is even an ironic twist. He may eventually use the endorsement, resources, and relationships of your biggest critics. The ones who rolled a boulder onto the road may be the very ones who remove the obstacles and provide your fuel for the journey. Isn't it just like God to turn the tables?

Obstacles can become opportunities, and adversaries can become advocates. Critics can become cheerleaders, and enemies can become emissaries. A setback can become a tremendous springboard for God's will. Take heart and keep your head up. It is darkest before the dawn. Hang in there with Jesus, and He will hold you up. Your Savior will sustain you. God's purposes will not be thwarted, so keep believing and watch Him work.

"Now finish the work, so that your eager willingness
to do it may be matched by your completion of
it, according to your means" (2 Corinthians 8:11).

Heavenly Father, I trust You to complete the work You have started in me. Strengthen me to do the work You have given me to complete.

Related Readings
Exodus 5:13; Nehemiah 2:18; Acts 14:26; Philippians 1:6; James 1:4

48

Ego's Snare

⊷

*Absalom's head got caught in the tree. He
was left hanging in midair, while the mule he
was riding kept on going…During his lifetime
Absalom had taken a pillar and erected it in the
King's Valley as a monument to himself.*

2 SAMUEL 18:9,18

An overinflated ego can hang you out to dry. It snares your soul
and shrivels your heart. Ego entwines a man's motives with self-
interest and self-credit. An ego has an insatiable desire for recognition
and power. It is sad to watch. Its need for accolades is an adolescent
attitude at its worst. An unchecked ego is an enemy that will lead you
down pitiful paths of regret. Left to its own devices, your ego will talk
you into things that feel good at the moment but end in humiliation.
An out-of-control ego exaggerates self-importance and creates conceit.

Conceit and Christ-centered living are mutually exclusive. I am
either letting Jesus call the shots or displaying Him as a facade for my
ego-infested life. Unless my Christian vocabulary and behavior are
void of ego, I am just using God to get my way for my benefit and my
glory. E-G-O stands for Edging God Out. It's all about me. Evangelists
driven by ego solicit converts for their own glory. Teachers motivated
by ego are shallow and sentimental even if their words are accurate
and deep. Leaders consumed by ego insist on having their way. Everyone recognizes ego's effect—except the one mastered by its deception.
Defuse ego's illusion with truth before it ruins your life.

Humility, accompanied by confession of your need for God and
people, will pin ego to the ground so you can walk unencumbered with
Christ. The Holy Spirit transforms a submitted ego and uses it for effective eternal results, so allow God to daily bend your ego toward Him.

Eventually, under His influence, you will develop habits that channel your energy into kingdom pursuits. You will finally experience joy in living through service to others and intimacy with your heavenly Father. Money, power, recognition, and control all fade in importance. What becomes valuable is pointing people to Jesus. You become motivated by mercy, humility, and justice.

Ego says yes to self; humility says no. Ego says yes to power; humility says no. Ego says yes to fame; humility says no. Ego says yes to always being right; humility says no. Ego says look at me; humility defers to Jesus. Ego erects monuments to man; humility builds the kingdom of God. Do not allow your ego to estrange you from eternity.

Die to your ego today and live for Christ. Seek out others with whom you can give and receive forgiveness. You can make the first move in forgiveness because you have nothing to lose and everything to gain. Pride feeds ego, and humility starves it. A short-term, earthly perspective makes room for ego, but an eternal perspective edges it out. Let Christ convert your ego from a liability to an asset.

"[Moses] regarded disgrace for the sake of Christ as of greater value than the treasures of Egypt, because he was looking ahead to his reward" (Hebrews 11:26).

Heavenly Father, I invite You to mold my soul into the image of Your Son Jesus Christ. By the power of Your Holy Spirit, I escort ego out, and I humbly depend on You.

Related Readings
Matthew 7:21; John 15:5; 2 Corinthians 6:18; Hebrews 12:5-6

49

Out-Serve

∞∞∞

*Now that I, your Lord and Teacher, have washed your feet,
you also should wash one another's feet. I have set you
an example that you should do as I have done for you.*

JOHN 13:14-15

Out-serve your wife. This is not natural to our selfish nature. But if you will out-serve your wife, you will start to see positive differences in both of you. She will feel cared for, and you will feel fulfilled. She will feel loved, and you will feel rewarded. She will feel respected, and you will feel significant. Of course, unappreciated service can wear you down over time, but trust God. Allow Him to supply the strength you need to serve. If the Lord is not empowering your service, you will eventually burn out and possibly become resentful. Bitter service does not last, but joyful service does.

Serve your wife out of gratitude to God for giving her to you. Serve her in the routines of life and when she least expects it. Serve her where she wants to be served, not just where you want to serve her. It may be unloading the dishwasher, taking out the garbage, mowing the lawn, maintaining the house, or taking care of the cars. Her service may include keeping the family organized, preparing dinner at home, being on time, keeping a calendar, or planning a trip. If you are unsure, ask her how she likes to be served.

Carry this attitude of out-serving into your occupation. Be a servant in the workplace, especially if you are a leader or manager. Quietly clean up the break room and wipe out the gooey microwave with its hodgepodge of flavors matted to the inside. Service from a sincere heart shows that you value and respect others.

Our Savior modeled service. He did not come to be served, but to serve and to give His own life in the ultimate act of service. When we enlist in the service of God's kingdom, we become His full-time servants. Service for the Savior is a thread that runs through the life of everyone who is led by the Lord. If Jesus is your model for leadership and for life, you will serve. He served the least and the greatest, sinners and saints, rich and poor. He served singles and families, the mad and the glad. He served when He was tired and when He was rested. You could not out-serve Jesus because His service was motivated and fueled by His heavenly Father. Intimacy with the Almighty compels you to serve.

Jesus served others even at the point of His greatest need. When engulfed in His own personal crisis, He chose to serve others and not to be served. The night before facing imminent death, He served by washing feet. Use this same selfless strategy of service and watch the world run to Jesus. In the middle of your own Last Supper experience, serve. When you are rejected, serve instead of retaliating. When you are forgotten, serve instead of feeling sorry for yourself. When you are hurt, serve instead of allowing your heart to harden. Serve for Jesus's sake and not your own. Make it a lifetime goal to out-serve everyone you come in contact with, especially those closest to you.

Out-serving others yields an outstanding outcome. An attitude of service is other-centered and Christ-focused. You can't out-serve Christ, but you can be a conduit of service on His behalf. Seek to out-serve others for your Savior.

—❦—

"The greatest among you will be your
servant" (Matthew 23:11).

Heavenly Father, I desire to follow the example of Jesus and serve others first.

Related Readings

Psalm 133:1; Romans 12:10; Philippians 2:3-4; 1 Peter 1:22; 5:5

50

Finish Well

◦◦◦

*Suppose one of you wants to build a tower. Won't
you first sit down and estimate the cost to see if
you have enough money to complete it? For if
you lay the foundation and are not able to finish it,
everyone who sees it will ridicule you, saying, "This
person began to build and wasn't able to finish."*

LUKE 14:28-30

Finishing well requires planning well. To plan well is to understand the cost of commitment. The commitment to follow Christ is not optional, but standard equipment for the Christian. To plan to finish well is to plan to follow Christ daily in humility and sacrifice. Finishing well tomorrow requires finishing well today. Finishing well does not imply a perfect life, but it requires a submitted life. This is a life that's under the authority of Jesus Christ, so finishing well is all about living as a committed disciple of Christ.

You may start your Christian life ablaze with the fire of your salvation, excited about your fresh new life, and contagious for Christ. However, unless you fuel your enthusiasm by understanding and applying God's Word, you will burn out. You will not finish well. People may even observe, "I thought you were a Christian. Didn't you used to attend church?" Finishing well is about joining with God to accomplish His will. Thus, finishing well is a building process. It is daily discerning God's best and then following Him wholeheartedly. Finishing well is a process that gradually takes shape. Your faithfulness gives you credibility to invest in others what you have learned. Out of your brokenness, you share with them what works and what doesn't work. You are more likely to finish well when you are pouring yourself into others, as that provides accountability.

You may have sons-in-law who are looking to you for leadership. You are one of their role models. Don't take this lightly. Your children and grandchildren will greatly benefit when you finish well. Pace yourself by God's grace so you can stay in the race until you make it to heaven. Finish well by becoming wiser today than you were yesterday. Love and forgive more today than you have in the past. This is the essence of finishing well. It is becoming more like Jesus in your attitude and actions.

Running this race of righteousness, we shed our sinful acts. Unrighteous anger is replaced with patience, and fear is replaced with trust. Pride is replaced with humility, and addictions are replaced with love. Be encouraged. If you are growing in Christ and building a life of obedience, you are finishing well.

You can finish well despite your soiled track record. God loves to rectify your false starts or your backsliding ways and place you on the road to finishing well. Stop today, turn from yourself, and turn to Christ. It is never too late to finish well. The wreckage from your past may still haunt you at times. But forget what is behind and press forward for the higher calling in Christ. He is your new reason for living. He is your life. He propels you forward to finish well. You will finish well for His sake, for your family's sake, and for the sake of others. By God's grace, plan to finish well, and you will.

—∞∞∞—

"After Job had prayed for his friends, the LORD restored his fortunes and gave him twice as much as he had before" (Job 42:10).

Heavenly Father, grow my daily desire to do Your will and finish well for Your glory.

Related Readings
Genesis 39:6-12; 1 Corinthians 9:24; Philippians 3:13-14;
   Hebrews 12:1-4

51

First Understand

*Fools find no pleasure in understanding
but delight in airing their own opinions.*

PROVERBS 18:2

Fools are quick to offer a cure before they understand the illness. That can be deadly. Offering medicine to someone who develops an allergic reaction could prove fatal. On the other hand, good advice is appropriate for the person and the situation. Anyone can offer an opinion, and fools love airing theirs. It is entertainment to them, for they delight in talking about anything as long as there is an opportunity to talk. However, a babbling fool can get you into trouble, so don't be impressed by his words. Instead, measure his words by making sure he understands you and your concern.

Look for time-tested principles, such as "Avoid disciplining your child in anger." The last thing you need is foolish advice based on an individual opinion. Look for wisdom from someone who looks you in the eyes with empathy. Take the time to validate their ideas from a variety of respected sources. Invite influence from those who draw their wisdom from the Word of God, and avoid people who talk too much. It is impossible to understand without listening. An unsure heart does not need a quick fix, but a listening ear. Those seeking wisdom need someone who listens with understanding.

So be very cautious in what you say and how you communicate your care. Ask, "Why do you want to do this? What does your wife think? Is this what you really want to do? What do you think God is telling you?"

Additionally, you can't go wrong by offering prayer support. The most appropriate counsel for you to offer may be to pray with the person seeking wisdom. Ask God to give them His divine counsel and directive. The wisdom of God, obtained in prayer, is the most valuable and accurate advice. Others will thank you for your wisdom when, in reality, you listened with understanding and empathy and then prayed with them for their discernment. Your advice may not sound as eloquent as a fool's self-serving soliloquy, but it is much more soothing for the soul.

Don't seek to impress others with your wise words. Instead, gain their trust and respect by truly seeking to understand their hopes and dreams. Learn what makes them afraid and what gives them peace. Find out where happiness and contentment reside for them. This level of intimate understanding gives you insight into their personality, temperament, and past experiences, and that will shed light on their present behavior. Wait to offer opinions until you thoroughly understand the person or situation. It's okay to wait. Wisdom comes to those who seek understanding first. Therefore, pray to see others as God does. Look for the good, and don't be naive about the bad.

Throughout your quest for understanding, continue to ask God what He thinks. Listen to Him, for the Lord's insight is understanding at its best.

———∞∞∞———

"Seek first his kingdom and his righteousness,
and all these things will be given to
you as well" (Matthew 6:33).

Heavenly Father, grow my patience so I will listen and understand before I offer advice.

Related Readings
Proverbs 2:2-9; 3:5-6; Colossians 1:9; James 1:19-20; 2 Peter 3:16

52

Considered Trustworthy

———— ∞ ————

*I thank Christ Jesus our Lord, who has
given me strength, that he considered me
trustworthy, appointing me to his service.*

1 TIMOTHY 1:12

God's primary prerequisite for service is trustworthiness. He is not looking for the most gifted, the most talented, the wealthiest, the most attractive, or the most popular. God is interested in bestowing His blessing on those who can be trusted.

Being in a position where God can trust you is a humbling place. His trust is both energizing and daunting. The God of the universe trusts you to implement His will for your life and to represent Him well through your good name and your faithfulness. He trusts you with His reputation, His truth, His children, His wisdom, His church, His Spirit, His work, and His kingdom.

You serve and love a trusting heavenly Father who enjoys extending Himself to those who can be trusted. Therefore, do not shrink back from God's trust. He has given you this opportunity because He trusts you. Your role is to represent Him responsibly, so be quick to give Him the credit for the success you are experiencing. Remain trustworthy, and continue to bathe each day in prayer and thanksgiving.

Seek wisdom and counsel from those who are wiser and more experienced than you, for a trustworthy individual is teachable. You are a lifetime learner who understands the need to grow. Education and experience are tools for developing and extending your trustworthiness. Daniel trusted God in the middle of his test. "The king was overjoyed and gave orders to lift Daniel out of the den. And when Daniel was lifted from the den, no wound was found on him, because he had trusted in his God" (Daniel 6:23).

People trust others who are trusted by God. The character quali-
ties that are attractive to God are the same traits that elicit the trust of
family, friends, and coworkers. Your good name is your most valuable
asset. Guard it with a God-fearing vigilance. People love and respect
you. This is a much greater honor than fame or fortune. People follow
those they trust.

"I want you to stress these things, so that those
who have trusted in God may be careful to devote
themselves to doing what is good. These things are
excellent and profitable for everyone" (Titus 3:8).

So let your life and actions—not just your words—prove you are
trustworthy. Do more than what's expected. Keep your word and follow
through. Attention to the little things builds big blessings. Above all else,
focus on being rather than doing. Be who you are in Christ, and the
proper doing will follow. In Christ, you are loved, accepted, forgiven,
and trusted. Trust Him and others, and you will be trusted by both.

"Here is a trustworthy saying: Whoever aspires to be
an overseer desires a noble task. Now the overseer is
to be above reproach, faithful to his wife, temperate,
self-controlled, respectable, hospitable, able to teach,
not given to drunkenness, not violent but gentle, not
quarrelsome, not a lover of money" (1 Timothy 3:1-3).

Heavenly Father, I desire to be Your trustworthy servant, whom
You can trust with Your blessings.

Related Readings
Exodus 18:21; Psalm 145:13; Luke 16:11-12; 19:17; 1 Timothy 1:15

53

Second Chances

Jesus straightened up and asked her...
"Has no one condemned you?"
"No one sir," she said.
"Then neither do I condemn you," Jesus
declared. "Go now and leave your life of sin."

JOHN 8:10-11

God is into second chances. You may not feel as if you deserve a second chance, and from a limited human perspective, you may not. This is the residue of sin. Sin, after it runs its course, leaves you in a distasteful position. You feel beat-up and used. You are embarrassed and ashamed. The only recourse seems to be to wallow in your guilt and shame while receiving verbal pelts from the "righteous." This is not where God wants you to remain.

Yes, sin brings guilt. Yes, there are those who will rub it in your face. Yes, sin brings consequences you may have to live with in this life and the next. Yet in Christ you are not condemned. You are not condemned! Christ was condemned on the cross for the crimes of mankind. He is your passageway to freedom from sin's condemnation.

This is the beauty of laying your life prostrate before Jesus. He does not pelt you with stones of self-righteousness. Instead, Jesus lifts up the broken sinner and puts him back together. He lifts you out of your unrighteousness and into His righteousness. Grace gives you a second chance.

We will all mess up. There is no doubt about this. But Lord willing, we will learn from our failures and not continue in sin. Confessing our sin and repenting brings freedom from condemnation. To be caught in sin and then continue in sin is condemnation. It is foolish. A fool gambles with God's patience. When confronted by God, capitulate. This is wisdom. Let Him lift you up, and then go and sin no more. There is no more condemnation in Christ.

There is a little bit of Pharisee in all of us—the condescending attitude that elevates us over the ones we condemn. This is the nature of pride. It is twisted in its motivation. I publicly criticize your sin to justify my private sin. But what is done in the darkness will come to light. It just takes time, and God is not limited by time.

Be quick to confess your own sin before judging other people's sin. This is a prerequisite. It is a big enough job to keep a clean account of one's own sins, much less try to manage the accounts of other people's sin. Most likely you do not have the time or expertise to take on someone else's sin management. Your example of confessing and repenting of your own sin will be much more helpful for them. By God's grace you can provide a safe environment for others to work through and exit their sin. Transparency leads to healing. Give others permission to be real.

Concealed sin kills, but repentance leads to healing. When people are hurting, hold back from hitting them over the head with the Bible. You will hurt one day and need acceptance for healing. Give others a second chance—God has done this for you and for them. Second chances are God's way. By following the way of God, everyone wins!

———— ✎ ————

"If we confess our sins, he is faithful and just
and will forgive us our sins and purify us
from all unrighteousness" (1 John 1:9).

Heavenly Father, thank You for giving second chances. Give me grace to do the same.

Related Readings

Jonah 2; Lamentations 3:21-23; John 3:17; Romans 8:1-2,34

54

A Wise Listener

—∞—

Listen now to me and I will give you some advice,
and may God be with you…Moses listened to
his father-in-law and did everything he said.

EXODUS 18:19,24

God sends people your way who offer great advice. Listen intently because you never know who may be speaking on behalf of God. You may trust these people, or you may not. Either way, do not allow pride to keep you from listening to what they say. Wisdom can come from the unlikeliest of sources, so listen with discernment. Wise listening requires thinking. The intent of wise listening is to separate the wheat from the chaff.

For example, you may be laboring away unnecessarily in stress and anxiety. Your stress may be self-inflicted. You may need a better system for processing people's needs. You may also be trapped in the never-ending cycle of busyness. Your life and organization are more complex than they were just six months ago. You need a better process for handling issues and complaints. People are starting to grumble. You're weary, and they are frustrated. The most obvious adjustment may be involving others to help you serve the people or the enterprise more effectively. Choose now to recruit and train others.

Do not try to talk your way out of your responsibilities. Rather, listen to those who are offering you advice and prayerfully consider their counsel. This may be the optimum time for you to let go and trust others. Your long-term security is not based on what you can control but on what you can give away.

Who in your life is currently offering you advice and counsel? Is it your wife, your father or father-in-law, or your mother or mother-in-law? Is it your boss, your employee, or your friend? Are you truly listening, or are you just going through the motions and not really adjusting or modifying your behavior?

There is a very good chance that the methods you have employed up to now will not propel you into the future. This time of uncertainty may provide a good opportunity to evaluate the basics of your life and work. What is the purpose? What do you do best? What is your capacity? Do you value quality over quantity? Do relationships have priority over tasks? What is your motive? This honest self-evaluation, coupled with the counsel of others, will help take you to the next level of living.

In addition, take time to listen to God. He offers clear guidance in the Holy Bible, and many, many times He speaks directly to you through other people's advice. Don't be afraid to ask someone, "What do you think?" Pray about the response and then value them and the Lord by acting on counsel that you believe is a word from God.

If you do not take the time for wise listening, you will succumb to foolish living. A wise listener is open to change. Without change for the better, we become worse. Listen, for God is speaking. This is wise and healthy living. Wise counsel continues for the wise listener, but it ceases for the one who chooses not to listen. We learn when we listen. God is "all about" advice and "all over" a wise listener!

"Let the wise listen and add to their learning,
and let the discerning get guidance" (Proverbs 1:5).

Heavenly Father, give me the patience and humility to listen more and talk less.

Related Readings
Exodus 14:14; Proverbs 12:15; Titus 3:1-2; James 1:19,22

55

Everyone's Battle

*I do not understand what I do. For what I want
to do I do not do, but what I hate I do.*

ROMANS 7:15

Everyone battles their own bad behavior. Becoming a Christian does not obliterate bad behavior. Becoming a Christian gives you the Spirit of Christ so you can choose good behavior. However, the battle still rages. We know the eternal war is won with our salvation in Christ, but the temporal battle with sin does not cease at salvation. We would be naive to think otherwise.

This spiritual warfare requires spiritual weapons. Fighting behavioral battles in your own strength leads to defeat. Do not be cocky with your Christianity. It is not a safety net for bad choices. Rather, it is the power of God for wise decision making. Still, the battle over bad behavior is a daily engagement.

You know you need to be patient, but you lose your temper instead. You know better than to covet another woman, but your lust lingers. You know you are to exercise forgiveness, but you harbor resentment. You look the other way when you should be humbly confronting. You lie when you know you should be honest and trust God with the outcome. Your pride and ego self-promote even though you know in your heart you should give God and others the credit and the glory. These conflicting behaviors do not go away. You find yourself feeling defeated because you once again gave in to behaving badly. How can this cycle cease?

The self-inflicted shame can drive you crazy. It can even lead you to give up on God. The battle over behavior is wearisome, but do not give in or give up. God cares. God understands. He is there with you moment by moment. In spite of behaving badly, you are not any less a Christian. And He does not love you any less. He feels for you in your conflicting emotions and actions. Most of the time He will not erase the negative consequences of your sin, but He will certainly stay with you during this disruptive time. God does not flee from your failures. He is there to help you pick up the pieces. He is there to help you learn from your mistakes. He equips and empowers you to win this behavioral battle in the future.

Do not be overwhelmed by the onslaught of the enemy on multiple fronts of your life. Fight these battles one at a time and watch God win. Seek out a mentor to coach you into wise living. Learn how to depend on the Spirit of God living through you. His grace is sufficient. He who lives in you is greater than he who lives in the world. No behavior, no matter how bad, can separate you from the love of your heavenly Father.

There is no condemnation in Christ Jesus. Start by being honest about the ugliness of the sin that continues to influence your attitude and behavior. Become more self-aware of blind spots that cripple your relational effectiveness. Learn how to live by faith and not by sight. Seek reconciliation with anyone you may have offended or who may have offended you. Avoid magazines and websites that flame your lust. These are everyone's battles, and they can be won. Fight with the weapons of God's wisdom and truth, not man's ingenuity. Let Him fight on your behalf. Be accountable to God and man. Move beyond the guilt of failure, and in Christ, enjoy freedom from condemnation. In Christ is everything we need to fight everyone's battle!

"I have told you these things, so that in me you may
have peace. In this world you will have trouble. But
take heart! I have overcome the world" (John 16:33).

Heavenly Father, in my struggles to do what's right, give me the strength and faith to follow Your will for my life.

Related Readings
Ecclesiastes 9:18; Jeremiah 1:19; 2 Corinthians 10:4; Philippians 4:13

56

God's Battle

The LORD does not deliver by sword or by spear; for the battle is the LORD's and He will give you into our hands.

1 SAMUEL 17:47 NASB

L ife is full of opportunities to do battle on behalf of the Lord. Engagement with fear is a spiritual skirmish waiting to happen, but the Spirit flushes out fear and defeats it with faith. Anger is always set to ambush and battle its foes, but patient forgiveness sees it coming and bypasses its ugly assault. Pride is lurking to pounce on the strong and successful, but humble prayer pushes back relentless reinforcements from hell. The enemies of God are brought down by God.

What battle are you facing that is getting the best of you? Is it a health issue? Cry out to Jesus, your Healer. Is it relational conflict? Submit to Christ, who can restore broken relationships. Perhaps you face a financial giant—go to God and seek godly counsel with transparency and trust, asking both for wisdom and accountability. Heaven provides the assistance you need through saints on earth. Look for the Lord's resources from those who love Him and you.

"Do not be afraid or discouraged because of this vast army. For the battle is not yours, but God's" (2 Chronicles 20:15).

Our true battle is not with the people or things we see, but with the unseen powers and principalities who seek to soil our faith in the Lord. The enemy, Satan, speaks lies to our minds, so we meander through life and struggle with feelings of insignificance. However, the truth of God dissolves the devil's deceptions and replaces them with clarity and confidence in Christ. The war in the heavenlies has already been won, so enlist in the Lord's army. Your battle is His battle.

Be bold as you wield your spiritual weapons. Depend on the Lord's wisdom and not the foolishness of man. Fire at obstacles with bullets of belief, not blanks of doubt. Shoot at the ultimate enemy, not at the messenger, who is only the bearer of bad news. Sling your smooth stone of spiritual service toward Satan. God directs your efforts to defeat the enemy!

———∞———

"The LORD will fight for you; you need
only to be still" (Exodus 14:14).

Lord Jesus, keep me engaged with Your Spirit and power as You go to battle for me.

Related Readings
1 Samuel 2:9; 2 Chronicles 14:11; Psalm 44:6-7; Hosea 1:7

57

The Source of Wealth

---

*You may say to yourself, "My power and the strength
of my hands have produced this wealth for me." But
remember the LORD your God, for it is he who gives
you the ability to produce wealth, and so confirms his
covenant, which he swore to your ancestors, as it is today.*

DEUTERONOMY 8:17-18

God is the source of wealth. He has the ability to give it and to take it away. We do not create our wealth—He does. We have skills, intelligence, and business acumen, but He gave us these things. We work hard, but He gave us the drive and the health to work hard. Wealth creation comes back to God.

He is the brains behind the operation. Whenever we forget this, we begin sliding toward pride and self-sufficiency. Depending on God was easier when you had nothing. If you now have more than you ever dreamed, you are probably tempted not to credit King Jesus with your wealth and resources. But He is not a silent or passive partner—you and your assets belong to Him. And as owner, He deserves and desires full disclosure of His powerful position.

So ask yourself, "How does God expect me to steward the wealth He has entrusted to me?" Of course it is not the "bigger barn" syndrome of lavishing all these resources on my wants and desires. Indeed, a good place to start is with the poor. The poor are prevalent in unprecedented numbers. However, their screams are silent, so they still lack the proper attention God desires. The poor are mostly out of sight and thus out of our mind, but Christ's heart breaks for them. His heart for the poor is "top of mind" for Him and should be for us as well. The poor do not deserve what is left over. They deserve "first dibs." We need to direct our frontline giving to the poor and needy. Rub elbows with the poor, and you will give to the poor!

Wealth is a huge responsibility not to be taken lightly. If you take credit for it, you have your reward. An earthly attitude toward wealth, without regard to God's heart, brings only an earthly reward. However, wealth invested and given to heavenly endeavors produces results and rewards way beyond this life. This is God's promise.

Pride facilitates spiritual amnesia. The less needy you become, the more you drift from your greatest source of life, Almighty God. In reality, the more you have, the more you need God. You can handle wealth well only with God's guidance. Otherwise, fear, greed, and pride will guide your decisions. God frees you to be generous and unleashes you to pursue kingdom initiatives.

So never forget that He is the source of your strength, the provider of your power, the wellspring of your wisdom, the artist of your abilities, and the underpinning of your wealth. You will be blessed when you are quick to give Him the credit for your success. Depend on Him in an independent environment, and your children will follow your example. Stay relentlessly reliant on your Savior and Lord. Then wealth remains a blessing and not a burden. Use the world's wealth as leverage for otherworldly purposes. This is confirmation of a growing relationship with Jesus Christ. So grow wealth and give wealth for His glory!

—⚬⚬⚬—

"The Lord sends poverty and wealth;
he humbles and he exalts" (1 Samuel 2:7).

Heavenly Father, I acknowledge You as my provider and the source of all good things in my life.

Related Readings

Deuteronomy 26:10; Proverbs 8:18; Hosea 2:8; Luke 16:11;
    1 Timothy 6:17-19

58

God-Sized Goals

———— ⌀⌀⌀ ————

*Jesus replied, "What is impossible with
man is possible with God."*

LUKE 18:27

God-sized goals challenge our thinking and further our faith. These Holy Spirit–inspired "big ideas" are crafted by our Creator to spur us on to good works and transformational living. God-sized goals make us uncomfortable at times. They are not guaranteed to happen, but they position us to pray more and believe in God better.

Through prayerful planning and implementation, gigantic goals are transformed from possibilities into probabilities. Huge objectives hedge against mediocrity and prod us toward perfection. God-sized goals are given to guide your thinking and your calendar so that you are intentional and focused on His big picture. Otherwise, you can drift about, destined for disappointment.

God-sized goals get you to God. Prayer, planning, and significant progress move you from the realm of possibility to the place of probability. In most cases, one man or woman's passion and focus drives the creation and execution of the goal. The leader looks failure in the face and defeats it by faith, wisdom, and hard work with the help of a skilled and unified team.

Christ-centered possibilities far outweigh man-centered probabilities. Perhaps you need to get away in solitude for several days, asking your Savior to sear your soul with His goals. Think outside the tiny box of unbelief, for the Lord's abilities and resources are unlimited. God-sized goals arrest your attention, adjust your attitude, and accelerate your actions.

So prayerfully set great goals, and God will grow your character in the process while influencing others for His glory. Trust Him to give you eyes of faith and to show you the way beyond the bounds of your experience, for His plan will prevail.

———∞———

"I know that you can do all things;
no purpose of yours can be thwarted" (Job 42:2).

What goal is God giving me that I need to accept in faith and work hard to accomplish?

Related Readings

Genesis 18:14; Jeremiah 32:17; Matthew 19:26; Ephesians 1:18-20

59

Good Versus Best

⸺⟩⟨⸺

*The Twelve gathered all the disciples together and
said, "It would not be right for us to neglect the ministry
of the word of God in order to wait on tables."*

ACTS 6:2

Many times, good is the enemy of the best. God's best is not always competing with gross sin or bad things. More often, you are distracted from your sweet spot by good things. Don't be lured into this approach to life. Everybody else's agenda for you does not necessarily equal God's agenda. Yes, the needs are great, but a need does not constitute a calling. This is where your courage and conviction can keep you from unwisely spreading yourself too thin. If you are scattered about in a multitude of activities, there is a good chance you will miss the opportunity to experience God's best.

Resist the temptation to be an inch deep and a mile wide. Rather, drill down into the divine call on your life. You know how you are wired and gifted. Validate what you do best with others who know you well. Tap into their wisdom and discernment. Your present predicament may be the result of overcommitment and inability. You can always tell when you are not operating in the vortex of your giftedness. Worthy and good activities become chores. Something haunts you. It is the realization that another talented person in this needed area could do a much better job than you with half the effort. It is sobering but true. So have the courage to find a replacement for this good activity so you can focus on what you do best.

Others admire what you do best. They celebrate your God-given skills. This is the role we all need to find for ourselves. Position yourself to excel in your clearest strength. Have the courage and the faith to say no to good people and good things. Mature people will understand.

Others may give you a hard time. But you can be at peace when you are immersed in God's best for you.

If you are a gifted teacher, do not be distracted by other opportunities that scream for your service. There are others who can serve but are unable to teach. In fact, a server might even aspire to teach because they value the outcome of helping people. But the amount of preparation and energy exerted toward this educational endeavor is not the best use of their time.

Choosing God's best often includes prioritizing important relationships over other endeavors. Children are children for a season. Watch their ball games instead of spending another hour at the office. Parents are parents for a finite period of time. Sit on the front porch with them and watch the grass grow—that's better than an occasional email or even a phone call.

Meeting a project deadline is strategic, but listening to a person in distress may be the greater priority. Do not dance with the good when the best is waiting in the wings. Dance with the best, and the good will take care of itself. God's role is to handle the good while you focus on the best. This is a step of faith, but you can trust God with the good and the best. Do not settle for the crumbs of the good. Instead, feast on the best!

"You must present as the LORD's portion
the best and holiest part of everything
given to you" (Numbers 18:29).

Heavenly Father, give me the faith to focus on Your best for me and not be lured away by other good opportunities.

Related Readings
Genesis 45:18; Ruth 3:3; Luke 15:22; Philippians 1:9-10;
    1 Thessalonians 3:1

60

Right Results, Wrong Methods

⌒⌒

*The LORD said to Moses... "Speak to that rock..." Moses
said to them, "Listen, you rebels, must we bring you water
out of this rock?" Then Moses raised his arm and struck
the rock twice with his staff. Water gushed out... But the
LORD said to Moses and Aaron, "Because you did not trust
in me to honor me as holy in the sight of the Israelites, you
will not bring this community into the land I give them."*

NUMBERS 20:7-12

Success is not measured by results. How you arrive at the results is even more important. Of course, results are important. But pragmatism is not king. Christ is King. He often cares about our methods more than our results.

A bad attitude leads to wrong methods. There is no getting around this. When people are ungrateful and immature, don't lash back at them. Cool off and pray rather than moving forward in anger. When you feel coerced, don't pout. Find your consolation in Christ and then make wise decisions. At home, don't blow up at your children or give in to their whining and complaining. This is a recipe for rebellion in their teenage years.

Fatigue and frustration are not conducive to wise decision making. Choose the best time to make important decisions and execute them. Negative emotions can be like a large, dull knife. They may get results but leave a jagged and bloody wound.

Before you launch into a direction of leadership, make sure you have a defined process of wise methods and accurate measurements. Create these with a calm and cool head. Do not act in a way that you later will regret. Previously planned processes are in place for your protection. These are checks and balances to assure excellence in execution.

God is focused on our methods. He expects to be honored and respected in the process as well as the results. If you run over people to reach your goal, you do not reflect the Lord you serve. However, if you serve people in the process of reaching the agreed-on goal, you illustrate the heart of Jesus.

So much hinges on our spirit, attitude, and actions. This trilogy can reflect right methods. Yes, methods need to be modified for efficiency and effectiveness, but this can be done through respectful dialogue rather than overbearing or callous dictating. Dignify people by explaining the rationale behind a change in procedures. The best ideas can come from those responsible to implement them. Listen keenly to the voice of reason. Wisdom resides here. You don't have to rush to get results out of fear of failure. You can wait, pray, and plan a process in collaboration with your team.

Work is sustainable when everyone is honored in the process. Focus on the right methods, and the right results will take care of themselves. Always remind yourself of how Christ would behave. The Spirit of Jesus cultivates the right attitudes and actions. Trust and honor God with the process and in the process. The right methods will support the right results!

"Whatever you do, work at it with all your
heart, as working for the Lord, not for
human masters" (Colossians 3:23).

Heavenly Father, purify my motives so I will do the right things in the right way at the right time for Your glory.

Related Readings

Isaiah 40:28-31; Matthew 6:1-4; 1 Corinthians 15:58;
    2 Corinthians 9:7

61

Power of the Path

—⁂—

*The angel of the L*ORD* [said]… "I have
come here to oppose you because your
path is a reckless one before me."*

NUMBERS 22:32

The path you choose is the path you use. It may be a path of pride or a path of humility. The path may stimulate purity or impurity. It could be a path of wisdom or a path of foolishness. The path may be one of cooperation or a path of independence. Your path may be family friendly or hostile to the health of your home.

Be careful how you seek after success because you can easily veer down the path of lost accountability. Make sure the path you traverse follows God's will. Your path is a picture of your pattern of choices. One after another, your daily decisions dig out a well-beaten path.

Do not be deceived—every path leads somewhere. Your current path is not insignificant. If it is a path of preparation, then prepare well. A well-prepared path paves the way for opportunity. But if you are not a good steward of your resources, relationships, finances, and skills, your future choices will be limited. Choose the path of patient preparation.

The more you prepare, the wider this path becomes. The path of preparation may seem long and onerous at times, but be patient and stay the course. Your faithfulness now will lead to influence later. Travel this path with focused attention. Enjoy the journey, for these may be the simplest days of your life. The path of preparation is the strong foundation of any excellent and eternally significant endeavor.

Also walk wisely on the path of personal intimacy with God. You can easily overlook this path because of familiarity or busyness. But without a well-worn path to God, you will wear out. It is a path that requires discipline, but the habit of exercising your faith now will serve you throughout your life. When you walk the path of intimacy with God, He fills you with His peace, security, and hope. This is not a path of quick fixes. Rather, it is one of trust and endurance. Traveling a path without God is like walking in the country on a moonless night. It's like running through a busy city during the day—blindfolded. In either case there is a lot of activity, but the activity is filled with fear, confusion, misdirection, and pain. The path of God may include some pain or uncertainty, but as you travel on His path, you are filled with His presence. The presence of God is peaceful. It is purifying and pleasing to the soul.

Life itself is one big path. If you travel alone, it is daunting. But with Christ, it is an adventure. The path of Christ is bumpy at times, but walking freely with Him is exhilarating. As you travel with God, be ever mindful of His guardrails of grace, love, and law. They are there for your protection. They keep you from straying off His path of kingdom purpose. The road most traveled is reckless compared to the less traveled path of heaven's security. Choose daily the wise path of confession and consultation with your Creator. The path of obedience to God leads to peace with God. He is a friend to be admired and a friend to be feared. When you stray, allow Him to lead you back. His path is what's best. Travel it with Him and travel it for Him!

⚬⚬⚬

"This is what the LORD says: 'Stand at the crossroads
and look; ask for the ancient paths, ask where
the good way is, and walk in it, and you will
find rest for your souls'" (Jeremiah 6:16).

Heavenly Father, keep me accountable to prayerfully stay on the path of Your will.

Related Readings
1 Kings 8:36; Psalm 119:3; Proverbs 12:15; Matthew 7:13-14; John 10:7

62

Time Management

～～～

Teach us to number our days,
that we may gain a heart of wisdom.

PSALM 90:12

Time can manage you, or you can manage time. Time can be elusive, or it can serve God's will for your life. Effective time management begins with teachableness—the admission that you need to learn how to better manage your time. If you do not manage your time well, you are not likely to manage your life well. Your life will become a series of reactions rather than a path of intentionality.

Managing time is like budgeting money. You have a limited amount, and you need to handle it wisely. A financial plan usually includes giving, investing, and spending. So it is with your time. You give back to the community with your volunteer work and service in the church. This is your giving of time in its purest form.

Your wisest investment is in people. Mentoring, coaching, counseling, and simply being a friend are common ways to invest in others. Investments in those who do not know Christ are especially valuable. The time you invest in unbelievers will be leveraged throughout eternity as they come to know Jesus.

And lastly, consider the wise spending of your time. This includes your daily usage—phone calls, meetings, emails, meals, and planning are all part of your time spent. Make sure this is not a mindless routine. Align your activities with your God-given purpose in life. If necessary, change your work environment or the way you spend your free time. Time is your most valuable asset. Manage it well, and you will seem to have more. This is God's way of redeeming the time!

Expert time management is a learned skill. Let God be your teacher. He created time, so He understands its intricacies. Time is finite, but its applications are infinite. Your wise use of time will create more capacity and minimize frustration. God will help you allocate and prioritize its use. He will instruct you if you ask Him. He dispenses His wisdom to all who take the time to listen. His wisdom will reveal your limitations—you cannot and should not do everything.

We all need the help of God and others. God's wisdom will lead you back to trust. Time management is a trust issue. You can trust God to provide just the right amount of time to accomplish His will. That's why you can implement the most important activities and trust Him with the things that do not seem to get done. Do you have a set deadline to leave work by six in the evening? When this self-imposed deadline rolls around, trust God with what is not yet done and go home to your family. This is priority living based on faith in God.

Every stage of life has its own priorities, so let God's Word and your trusted advisors help you define your areas of focus. Allow room for interruptions. It is naive to think your time allocations will work flawlessly each day. Life happens. People need things that are not on the agenda for that day or meeting. Allow for breaks between appointments because inevitably, people run late or meetings run over.

Each day is a gift from God. Take the time to manage your time!

<hr>

"Why, you do not even know what will happen
tomorrow. What is your life? You are a mist that
appears for a little while and then vanishes.
Instead, you ought to say, 'If it is the Lord's will, we
will live and do this or that'" (James 4:14-15).

Heavenly Father, I trust You to provide the needed amount of time to do Your will.

Related Readings
Psalm 139:16; Proverbs 16:9; 27:1; Isaiah 2:22; Luke 12:18-20

63

Morning Preparation

In the morning, LORD, you hear my voice;
in the morning I lay my requests before you
and wait expectantly.

PSALM 5:3

Start the day with God. This is your best preparation. The morning is the best part of the day. Appointments have yet to assault your calendar. Interruptions are blocked from your schedule. Each day is full of new opportunities and challenges.

Because each day is unique, we need a daily dose of God. We need His wisdom, His forgiveness, and His perspective. Just as our body needs exercising and bathing, so our mind, soul, and heart need God's cleansing and renewal. Time with God feeds our soul like a nice meal nourishes our body.

Is spending time with God a struggle for you? Perhaps you are moving too quickly. Slow down your pace, or He may slow it down for you. If you have rested well the night before, your mind and body are the most receptive in the morning. Using this pliable time of the day to recalibrate with God makes good sense. "First in, first out" is a good description of what happens in the morning. If the worries of the world consume the beginning of our day, then worry will come out first during the day. If trust in God fills our first moments, then trust will come out first during the day.

Jesus modeled this for us as He rose before the day and began to spend time with His heavenly Father. Find a quiet spot with the fewest distractions so you can listen intently to your heavenly Father. Wake up with God while the world sleeps. Then, when the world awakes, you can greet it with grace and truth. Your time with God need not be complicated. Converse just as you do daily with close friends; keep the dialogue honest and open. God already knows our heart, but we forget and need a reminder. My heart deceives me, but God cuts through the deception and gets to the core of the matter.

My anger may cause me to sin by not letting go of a person or a situation. Letting go and trusting God with the matter can be difficult. But you cannot blame another for your bad attitude—this is between you and God. Ask Him to do an attitude check and to fill your "gratitude tank" before you run out of gas. If gratitude is not motivating your living, you will burn through energy like dry firewood on a blistering cold winter night. Without daily doses of divine gratitude, your enthusiasm will float away like smoke up a chimney.

The morning is an ideal time to lay our requests before our heavenly Father. When you walk close with God, the desires of your heart will align more closely with His wishes for your life. This is reassuring. As you walk with Jesus each day, ask Him by faith for a pure heart. Ask Him to lead you to the right career opportunity in His timing. Look to Him for courage to walk away from a relationship or a deal or to accept a new challenge—one that forces you out of your comfort zone. Ask Him for the trust and the patience to accept His timing with all the issues crowding your mind. There is no better way to start your day than with God!

―――⚬⚭⚬―――

"Very early in the morning, while it was still dark,
Jesus got up, left the house and went off to a
solitary place, where he prayed" (Mark 1:35).

Heavenly Father, wake me in the morning to start my day with You in listening prayer.

Related Readings
Psalms 5:3; 88:13; 119:147; 143:8; Isaiah 50:4; Luke 11:1; Acts 16:13

64

Presumptive Praying

*They soon forgot what he had done
and did not wait for his plan to unfold.
In the desert they gave in to their craving;
in the wilderness they put God to the test.
So he gave them what they asked for,
but sent a wasting disease upon them.*

PSALM 106:13-15

Be careful what you pray for—you may receive it and more, and it may not be pleasant! Prayer is not a magic wand you can use to make all things better. God is not a genie who resides in a magic lamp, waiting at your beck and call. Our prayers don't constrain Him to grant our wishes. But sometimes we drift into this presumptive way of thinking. We begin to take God for granted. And when things do not go to our liking, we ask God to bail us out or to intervene on our behalf. Somehow the issue always comes back to control—*our* control.

God can handle any situation, so why try to force the issue? Part of the answer is fatigue. When we are emotionally, physically, or spiritually spent, we do not make the best decisions. We ask for what we should not ask for. We do what we should not do. Our praying becomes presumptuous rather than humble, grateful, and patient. Presumptive prayers want a quick fix and a quick out. We are duped into thinking that God owes us this opportunity or relief. If we are persistent in our self-preserving attitude of praying, we may get what we're asking for. But our will is a cheap substitute for His.

Patient praying, on the other hand, is Christ-centered. Through it we trust God to perform His will, not ours. It is a reassuring way to pray. The weight of the world does not rest on our way of doing things. God can and will handle things in His timing. We shift from a demanding spirit to a dependent spirit. We truly trust that God has our best interests in mind. He does not need to be conjured or convinced. Prayer aligns our hearts with God's heart, not His with ours (that is a scary thought).

Patient praying includes searching the Scriptures to review good examples of prayer. As you learn, your prayers grow in accuracy and authenticity. Prayer is an awesome responsibility not to be taken lightly or flippantly. God delights in answering prayers that align with His character and purposes. This is who He is. This is what He does. Be prayerful. Be other-centered in your praying. Seek His face first, not His hand. Pray from a pure heart and a humble head. Patient praying beats presumptive praying every time. It is the way to go. It works. So be careful what you pray for. You may get it and more.

"Brothers and sisters, my heart's desire
and prayer to God for the Israelites is that
they may be saved" (Romans 10:1).

Heavenly Father, protect me from presumptive prayers and teach me to pray in humble dependence on You.

Related Readings

Exodus 17:2; Numbers 14:40-45; Matthew 6:5; Mark 11:17;
    1 Corinthians 10:9

65

God Audit

Search me, O God, and know my heart;
test me and know my anxious thoughts.
See if there is any offensive way in me,
and lead me in the way everlasting.

PSALM 139:23-24

Expect God to conduct a regular audit of your life. His Holy Spirit is an expert at probing beneath the surface of our actions and rooting out unhealthy motives and habits. We can talk ourselves into anything, but God holds our feet to the fire of His expectation.

He searches our hearts, looking for payouts of forgiveness to others. Keep your relational accounts short. In Christ, you can forgive others of their debt. Write off their offenses, and you will enjoy heavenly credits. This is what we do as Christians—we forgive. We forgive because of the great mercy we have received from our heavenly Father.

Another common discovery from God's audit is fear. Our minds swirl with scenarios out of our control. Fear of failure, fear of confrontation, fear of rejection, and fear of the future can immobilize you. These fears birth anxious thoughts that refuse to go away.

God's probing will put a finger on your worries, and He will remind you to trust Him. He gently and lovingly says not to let anxiety drive you, but to trust. He can handle anything He uncovers in your life and anything you encounter in life. This is what He does as God. He calms you during uncertainty and stabilizes you in difficult circumstances. Trust your heavenly auditor—whatever He asks you to change will be for your good and the good of others. His audit is for your benefit.

This divine accounting of your life is based on your invitation. Yes, the Holy Spirit is performing an internal audit at all times. As a follower of Jesus Christ, you can never get away from His prompting, convicting, and comforting presence. He is ever at work—even when you are unaware. But busyness can barricade you from the Holy Spirit's influence. You can run so hard that you run right by His warning signs. Your wife says to slow down, or you see the children growing up without you, but you keep running. Your body screams to slow down, but you keep running—until your first heart attack. Your schedule says to slow down, but you keep breaking promises and letting people down.

God's audit may require you to go away and open the books of your life to the life giver Himself. Trust that things will go just fine as you take the time to listen to your heavenly auditor. Listen intently and obey. This pause in your schedule is meant to propel you forward. A time of introspection, confession, and repentance frees you to move ahead in the power of the Holy Spirit. Your freedom and opportunities will multiply when you are God-compliant. Clean books and a clear conscience expand your capacity and energize you for God's next assignment.

———— ∞ ————

"The LORD does not look at the things people look at. People look at the outward appearance, but the LORD looks at the heart" (1 Samuel 16:7).

Heavenly Father, search my heart, purify my motives, and make me more like Christ.

Related Readings
1 Chronicles 29:17; Psalm 7:9; Proverbs 17:3; Jeremiah 11:20;
    Revelation 2:23

66

Career Challenges

❈

Whatever you do, work at it with all your heart, as
working for the Lord, not for human masters.

COLOSSIANS 3:23

Career challenges are meant to keep us close to Christ, not drive us
to default to our own drive and determination. The fear of layoffs,
downsizing, and restructuring can linger over our lives like a bad dream.
Our confidence is shaken as we wonder if we will continue to receive
a paycheck. We may feel extremely vulnerable because our industry is
caught up in change and consolidation.

However, these down cycles are your opportunity to remain a
dependable employee, partner, investor, or boss. For instance, make
sure your attitude aligns around the Almighty's big picture for your
life. This season of service has been a gift from your Savior, and going
forward, you are a much better person than before. Use these days of
uncertainty to stay engaged in your job. Remain an asset rather than a
liability to your company. Your work is for the Lord first, so labor with
passion, focus, and diligence.

There are various ways to keep a stellar testimony during these trying times at the office. First, focus on doing your job with excellence,
and don't allow fear to force you into an early exit. Sometimes you feel
conflicted, just as Nehemiah did—you are building the wall with half
your resources and fighting the enemy of discouragement with the
other half (Nehemiah 4:17).

Second, be flexible as people leave. You may need to take on some
new responsibilities. See this as an opportunity to expand your capacity and learning. Your boss remembers who worked harder and smarter
during the hard times. Be willing to get out of your comfort zone and

serve in a totally new role if that is what it takes to weather your current vocational storm.

––––∞––––

> "Do you see someone skilled in their work?
>   They will serve before kings;
>   they will not serve before officials of low rank"
>   (Proverbs 22:29).

Lastly, if you are a supervisor, manager, director, or executive team member, do the right thing the right way and trust God with the results. Stay under the authority of wise objective counsel and follow through on their advice. Make the hard call early to let someone go, but do it with grace and generosity. Pray with and for the team member you ask to exit. Look them in the eye and affirm their contribution to the organization. Do everything you can in good conscience to provide them contract work or connect them with other career opportunities.

Christians have a responsibility to reach out to those in transition and to walk additional miles with them in their search for work (Matthew 5:41). The way you manage is your ministry, so take it seriously and prayerfully. Your career constituents are your congregation—they need to see you model Christ in the marketplace. Men and women are most vulnerable and teachable in the middle of career challenges and transitions, so use this window of ministry to love them toward the Lord. Career challenges are meant to draw everyone closer to Christ!

––––∞––––

> "So that everyone he has made may know his work,
>   he stops all people from their labor" (Job 37:7).

How can I best model Christ in my current career challenge?

Related Readings

2 Chronicles 34:12; Nehemiah 5:15; Psalm 127:1; 1 Timothy 4:10

67

Effective Accountability

———— ∞ ————

As iron sharpens iron,
so one person sharpens another.

PROVERBS 27:17

Accountability is essential for the follower of Jesus Christ. We are accountable to God and man. Accountability brings integrity to our commitments and follow-through in God's will for our lives. We all do better when others are watching.

The details of your life may be blurry to most. But when you surround yourself with trusted advisers, you give them the reading glasses to your heart and soul. They see and understand your motives—the good and the bad reasons why you do what you do. In a supportive and safe environment, you share with them your struggles, sins, and fears.

Accountability slows you down. It takes time to consider hard questions about your time in prayer and God's Word, your thought life, your financial health, your marriage, your work, your schedule, and so on. Nothing is off-limits when you are truly accountable. Accountability is most effective when you sincerely submit to others.

Collaboration and a small group perspective can provide you with a 360-degree evaluation. Find a small group of four or five who are willing to grow old with you—people who can tell when you're blowing smoke. Men who can read you because they really know you. They know your tendency to drink too much, to blow up in a fit of rage, or to take your wife for granted. They know how your unguarded strength can become your greatest weakness. They help you keep these pitfalls in check.

They also affirm your progress and success. Accountability includes positive reinforcement as well as warning or rebuke.

True accountability partners point you to God. He is the standard.

His Word holds the rules of the game. When an issue is under debate, biblical principles trump other considerations. Submission and obedience to God are the foundation and the goal of accountability. He is still there when no one is watching. He understands the motives of our hearts when we ourselves are confused.

Fear of God is good and effective accountability. When you fear the Lord, what you say and do matters for today and for eternity. Your respect and love for Him become so strong that you want to do His will no matter what. Your desire to grow in His character drives your life. This type of God-conscious living grows your accountability over time. You discover more of God's expectations for your life—expectations you never knew existed. You also become free of some limits on your life that you have imposed but God never intended.

Effective accountability with God requires time and transparency. Seek His face and ask what needs to change in your life. Let others know what God is teaching you and ask for their mutual accountability. Submit to God, caring friends, and your wife. Accountability leads to freedom. Be set free!

―∞―

"So then, each of us will give an account of ourselves to God" (Romans 14:12).

Heavenly Father, I want to be transparent and real with a small group of trusted friends who can love me and encourage me in Your ways.

Related Readings

Luke 17:3; Galatians 6:1-5; 1 Thessalonians 5:11; Hebrews 4:13; James 5:16

68

Financial Accountability

*We want to avoid any criticism of the way we administer
this liberal gift. For we are taking pains to do what is right,
not only in the eyes of the Lord but also in the eyes of man.*

2 CORINTHIANS 8:20-21

Financial accountability is of primary importance to an organization with integrity. This especially applies to gifts made in the name of the Lord to a church or ministry. Those who name the name of Christ must maintain a high standard of fiduciary responsibility. Cavalier money managers are suspect, but conscientious stewards establish a reputation of wise financial management.

What checks and balances does your church have in place to protect you from fraud? Are the ministries you support audited by outside firms to assure impartial oversight? These are basic, bottom-line best practices that protect everyone involved. Naive trust without financial accountability can lead to mismanagement of funds.

Wise money managers don't do just enough to get by. They go the extra mile to avoid any criticism of their appropriation of funds. They make a solemn commitment to steward well the Lord's resources. Churches and ministries that highly value stewardship go to great pains to put in place leaders of integrity—men and women who manage money with honesty.

How are your personal finances? Has God blessed you materially? Do you represent Him well as His money manager? Is a financial professional of good character looking over your shoulder to provide accountability? Secretive financial practices invite suspicion, but full financial disclosure offers clarity.

If you are married, financial ignorance is not an option. One spouse may manage the finances, but the other needs to understand their financial status, and they need to hold each other accountable. Most families and organizations do not complain of too much financial accountability, but many get in trouble where it's lacking.

Therefore, whether at work, home, or church, implement financial processes and policies that provide ongoing accountability. Those who manage well will be blessed with more. Passing the small tests in financial accountability affords you larger opportunities later on. Honor the Lord and man by taking pains to be financially accountable.

———❧———

"Well done, good and faithful servant! You have been faithful with a few things; I will put you in charge of many things" (Matthew 25:23).

How can I be a catalyst for financial accountability at work, home, and church?

Related Readings
Judges 17:2; Amos 8:5; Matthew 27:3-5; 1 Corinthians 16:1-4

69

Temptation's Allure

*When the woman saw that the fruit of the tree was good
for food and pleasing to the eye, and also desirable for
gaining wisdom, she took some and ate it. She also gave
some to her husband, who was with her, and he ate it.*

GENESIS 3:6

Temptation is not ugly. It is attractive. It wears seductive cloth-ing and alluring perfume. A smiling and bubbly woman who brings energy and a little too much excitement into a business rela-tionship, luscious meals with way too many calories, a no-lose finan-cial deal that's a bit sketchy…these things and so many more bait our unguarded appetites.

We cannot feed our bodies large quantities of poor-quality food without consequences. So don't live to eat, but eat to live. Good health is a gift from God. Steward it well and wisely. Budget your diet as you do your money. Your physical well-being is one of your best invest-ments. Better to pay a personal trainer now than a surgeon later.

The same goes for your optical intake. Don't allow your eyes to feast on someone or something you cannot have. Why place yourself in a position of compromise? If you travel, hire an intern of the same sex for accountability and apprenticeship. You may need to remove your television or computer from your home for a season so you aren't bom-barded by temptation. Appreciate the beauty your eyes behold, but do not desire or crave its object.

Use your finances to care for your family and promote the kingdom of God. Establish best practices in your professional and personal stew-ardship. Enjoy the blessings God has given you and bless others as He enables you. You'll experience more joy in giving than you could ever know simply by getting.

Temptation won't go away until we go to glory. It started in the Garden of Eden, and it continues today. Even in the best of environments, temptation crouches at the door. There is no completely encapsulated temptation-free zone. However, you can be smart and avoid situations that feed and facilitate temptation. You may need to break off a friendship or quit confiding in a coworker about your marital problems (seek professional help instead). Innocent flirting can easily lead to infidelity.

Temptation is a fire waiting to destroy. Do not go close to its flickering flames. Instead, draw closer to the warmth of God's love and to those who love you the most. When you are frustrated, you are more likely to fall into temptation, but reject this excuse. Invite the Holy Spirit to douse temptation's fires. Let people who care know what you are thinking and doing. We do better when others are watching. The consequences of giving in to temptation are crushing. The fruit of following Jesus is rich, rewarding, and satisfying. Reject the tempter and accept your Savior Jesus. Never forget—the bait has a hook!

———— ∞ ————

"Lead us not into temptation, but deliver
us from the evil one" (Matthew 6:13).

Heavenly Father, through my love for You and my fear of sin's consequences, deliver me from the deceptions of the evil one.

Related Readings
Matthew 4:1; 26:41; Luke 11:4; 1 Corinthians 10:13; James 1:13-15

70

Trials and Temptations

◦◦◦

*No temptation has overtaken you except what
is common to mankind. And God is faithful; he
will not let you be tempted beyond what you
can bear. But when you are tempted, he will also
provide a way out so that you can endure it.*

1 Corinthians 10:13

What is temptation? It is desire enticing you to make an unwise decision. To be tempted is not a sin, but it does reveal that a sinful desire is being conceived. We are wise to see temptation coming and prepare to overcome its deceitful power. Trials are outward tests that can lead to inward temptations. When weakened by adversity, we become prime targets of our adversary, the devil. So how can we be prepared to overcome trials and temptations?

A job promotion can be a good thing, but what if it requires the test of travel? Time away from home cannot be properly replaced by any amount of money. And what are the agreed-on guidelines (with ourselves and, if we are married, with our wife) to keep us from falling into temptation? The moral temptation is to not remain faithful. The ethical temptation is to compromise our honesty. Peer temptation is to give into juvenile behavior. Intentional preplanning is the best way to deal with temptation. Avoid compromising situations. Don't be alone with the opposite sex, avoid nightclubs, and keep accurate expense reports.

◦◦◦

"Each person is tempted when they are dragged away
by their own evil desire and enticed. Then, after desire
has conceived, it gives birth to sin; and sin, when it
is full-grown, gives birth to death" (James 1:14-15).

Many people desire to get rich. Wealth is tempting because of the allure of affluence—freedom, nice homes, new cars, power, and prestige. The test of prosperity calls for a generous spirit. Otherwise, money creates its own idols. Those blessed materially learn how to leverage their possessions for God's kingdom and not their own. They recognize the Lord as the owner and themselves as stewards. Generosity trumps the temptation of greediness.

Use trials to draw closer to Christ. Avoid the temptation to pull away from Him. Don't allow hard times to harden your heart. Instead, invite the Spirit to soften your heart. Alone in the desert, Jesus was tempted by the devil, but He answered Satan's lies with the truth of Scripture. So seek the Lord when He seems distant, and He will draw you to Himself. Be transparent with mentors and friends who can support you in remaining faithful. Confessing your vulnerabilities weakens temptation's grip. Christ provides a way of escape for patient endurance.

"Because he himself [Jesus] suffered when he was tempted, he is able to help those who are being tempted" (Hebrews 2:18).

Heavenly Father, lead me away from temptations and into the joy of doing Your will.

Related Readings

Job 1:12; Matthew 4:1; 6:13; 1 Timothy 6:9; Hebrews 4:15; James 1:13-15

71

Prayer and Action

We prayed to our God and posted a guard
day and night to meet this threat.

NEHEMIAH 4:9

Prayer does not preclude action, and action does not dismiss prayer. Being and doing are necessary for partnering with God's will. Nehemiah and his team tethered their hearts to God in trust, but they also assigned a guard 24/7 to watch out for attacks from the enemy. Yes indeed, prayer empowers the person praying to be bold in the work of God. It produces an inner resolve to serve as to the Lord. Prayer and watchfulness work together to accomplish the Almighty's purposes.

What tension do you feel between doing your part and trusting God to do His part? Wisdom seeks Christ daily to determine how He is leading. His Holy Spirit will guide you in what needs to be done for today. Don't allow unnecessary interruptions to rob you of experiencing God's best. Beware of those who live frantic and faithless lives. Their problems need not become your crises lest you are led astray. Pray for needy people and help them as the Spirit leads. Watch out for distractions.

"But Martha was distracted by all the preparations that had to be made. She came to him and asked, 'Lord, don't you care that my sister has left me to do the work by myself? Tell her to help me!'" (Luke 10:40).

Prayer produces the right actions. Activities without insight from Almighty God can miss being the most effective. Just as a sailor on deck looks up to the captain on the bridge for a clearer view, so we are wise to peer into the Lord's perspective as our guide before moving forward. Heaven's telescope of truth is able to focus in on what needs to happen on earth. When we seek wisdom from above, we better understand what to do below. Actions led by prayer get the best results.

What are you facing that invites prayer and support from other saints of God? Whom can you summon into your confidence for comfort, love, and intercession? Signs of trouble aren't meant to be faced alone, but in the strength of the Spirit and undergirded by a caring community. You may be used to assisting others, but now is your opportunity to receive. Believers are blessed when they can be a blessing to you. The body of Christ is healthy when it prays and acts in love toward one another.

"Pray that the LORD your God will tell us where we should go and what we should do" (Jeremiah 42:3).

Heavenly Father, I pray You will lead me in where I should go and in what I should do.

Related Readings

Jeremiah 42:20; Daniel 6:10; Matthew 6:5-7; Acts 9:40;
      2 Corinthians 13:7

72

Management Complements Leadership

———— ∞ ————

*[Jesus] directed the people to sit down on the
grass. Taking the five loaves and the two fish and
looking up to heaven, he gave thanks and broke
the loaves. Then he gave them to the disciples,
and the disciples gave them to the people.*

Matthew 14:19

Jesus was a leader worth following. He was also a manager who managed well. He understood the importance of an orderly process, and He implemented it effectively. Leadership ensures the enterprise is on the right strategic path, and management is the method for executing the mission. Leadership will languish without good management moving critical initiatives forward.

Wise managers clearly define who, what, when, where, and how. Their attention to detail supports the team's objectives. Managers diagnose problems and bring solutions to bear. They remove obstacles and reclaim progress. Managers implement methods that support the success of the organization. Like the Lord in His creation, they bring order and discipline to the enterprise.

———— ∞ ————

"Dominion and awe belong to God;
  he establishes order in the heights of heaven"
    (Job 25:2).

Successful managers are almost obsessive about clear communication and mission-critical measurements. They constantly ask, does the team understand their responsibilities? Are the schedule and deadline clear? How can we be better at what we do? What are the leading indicators telling us, and how do we need to adjust?

As a manager, you are a steward of God's time, money, and resources at home and at work. So seek the Owner for His wisdom. Make sure you know how He expects you to treat people and oversee the process. Good managers make people their priority while still managing below budget. Your task may seem impossible, but you can trust the Lord to multiply your efforts and resources in creative and innovative ways. Stay faithful to manage well, and you will be in a position to be entrusted with much more.

"Well done, my good and faithful servant. You have been faithful in handling this small amount, so now I will give you many more responsibilities. Let's celebrate together!" (Matthew 25:21 NLT).

How would I improve as a manager if I served people more at their point of need?

Related Readings
Genesis 39:2-6; Nehemiah 2:11-20; Luke 12:42; 16:1-8

73

God's Favor

*When his master saw that the LORD was with him
and that the LORD gave him success in everything he
did, Joseph found favor in his eyes and became his
attendant. Potiphar put him in charge of his household,
and he entrusted to his care everything he owned.*

GENESIS 39:3-4

The Lord's favor rests on His followers who remain faithful to Him. It is humbling to know that God extends wisdom and grace to those who go after Him with all they've got. We may be separated from our loved ones by distance, but the Lord is always nearby, imparting His calming presence. Rest assured, Jesus brings success to souls who submit to His will.

Favor with God leads to favor with man. You are much more likely to connect with people's hearts on earth when you have connected with God's heart in heaven. People of influence are on the lookout for those whom they can trust. It is not a small thing to delegate management and leadership responsibilities, and those with proven character are entrusted with more.

"Whoever can be trusted with very little can also be
trusted with much, and whoever is dishonest with very
little will also be dishonest with much" (Luke 16:10).

Be faithful in your responsibilities as a servant leader at work and home. Maintain a joyful attitude in difficult situations, and Jesus will bless you. Your boss may be unreasonable, your spouse insensitive, or your child disrespectful, but the Lord will see your humble heart and reward you with respect, responsibility, and rest.

What are you to do when God prospers you and your family? What are His eternal expectations? Certainly the Lord looks for His glory to be revealed through a life that reflects praise and thanksgiving. When we smash the idols of materialism, sex, and power—replacing them with modest living, love, and service—people want to know why. Questions about our "peculiar" lifestyle are meant to point people to Jesus.

—∞—

"Dear friends, I urge you, as foreigners and exiles,
to abstain from sinful desires, which wage war
against your soul. Live such good lives among the
pagans that, though they accuse you of doing
wrong, they may see your good deeds and glorify
God on the day he visits us" (1 Peter 2:11-12).

So instead of seeking the world's favor, submit to God's authority, and His favor will follow. God will bless your life when you love the Lord and people. As the moon is a reflection of the sun's light, you can be a reflection of the Son's light, illuminating the Lord's ways to wayward souls. The Lord is on the lookout to extend His blessings on those who fear Him, trust Jesus, and love people.

—∞—

"The Lord's hand was with them, and a great number of
people believed and turned to the Lord" (Acts 11:21).

Am I in a position of humble obedience and trust so I can experience the favor of God?

Related Readings

1 Chronicles 28:19; Isaiah 62:3; Luke 1:66; 1 John 2:8-10

74

Confidence in Leadership

—————⚬⚬⚬—————

*Have confidence in your leaders and submit to their
authority, because they keep watch over you as those who
must give an account. Do this so that their work will be a
joy, not a burden, for that would be of no benefit to you.*

HEBREWS **13:17**

Leaders must win people's confidence if they are to maintain credibility. When confidence is lost, creditability is not far behind, and influence is forfeited. A leader's role invites confidence from others, but the leader must consistently display a strong character and effective results to maintain the status of a trusted advisor.

Are you a leader worth following? Do your wife and children have confidence in your decision-making process? Do they see a spiritual leader who follows the Lord well? If so, you have the benefit of being held in high esteem and considered trustworthy. People willingly follow leaders who establish appropriate accountability systems.

—————⚬⚬⚬—————

"David said to God, 'Was it not I who ordered the
fighting men to be counted? I, the shepherd, have
sinned and done wrong. These are but sheep. What
have they done? LORD my God, let your hand fall
on me and my family, but do not let this plague
remain on your people'" (1 Chronicles 21:17).

Ministers of the gospel of Jesus Christ are on display as they model belief and behavior. The bar is set high—they are accountable to Almighty God for how they represent His kingdom. Leaders for the Lord demonstrate the Christian trademark—loving well. To love well means to listen to criticism in order to grow personally. To love well is to comfort the afflicted with the balm of grace. To love well is to challenge a changing world with unchanging truth.

When followers of Jesus see their pastor follow Jesus with a humble heart, a disciplined mind, and a lifestyle of accountability, they are reassured and secure. When leaders and followers desire to do the Lord's will and trust each other, the relationship is filled with joy and peace. The burden of leading grows lighter when the leader is confident in Christ.

"Keep watch over yourselves and all the flock of
which the Holy Spirit has made you overseers.
Be shepherds of the church of God, which he
bought with his own blood" (Acts 20:28).

So seek to be a loving leader who wins the confidence of those you serve. As one who ultimately follows Christ first, submit to those in authority over you (whether they deserve it or not) and trust that the Lord will hold them accountable to His standards.

"Now may the God of peace, who through the blood of
the eternal covenant brought back from the dead our Lord
Jesus, that great Shepherd of the sheep, equip you with
everything good for doing his will, and may he work in us
what is pleasing to him, through Jesus Christ, to whom
be glory for ever and ever. Amen" (Hebrews 13:20-21).

What authority do I need to submit to as I maintain confidence in Christ, trusting He will hold them accountable to His standards?

Related Readings
Ezekiel 34:10; John 10:11-12; Romans 3:19

75

Sought by God

⸺◦⊷◦⸺

*Now your kingdom will not endure; the LORD
has sought out a man after his own heart and
appointed him ruler of his people, because
you have not kept the LORD's command.*

1 SAMUEL 13:14

God seeks men and women who are sensitive to His heart. Saul, motivated by pride and fear, did not keep the Lord's command, so God appointed David as the next king. A leader risks losing the Lord's respect when he disrespects the Lord's commands. Believers lose their positive influence on people when their influence with the Almighty wanes. God seeks sincere seekers with whom He can entrust His favor. He recruits team players who will learn His system and adapt to it.

Have you become too familiar with your heavenly Father and His commands? Has your familiarity begun to breed contempt? If so, you can be restored through grace-based obedience, or you can risk losing your position of authority. Let your heart rest in the hand of your heavenly Father. You will endure under the mighty hand of God, but if you are out from under His authority, your hope will shrivel and His help will fade away. So submit to His authority.

⸺◦⊷◦⸺

"For the eyes of the LORD run to and fro throughout
the whole earth, to show Himself strong on behalf
of those whose heart is loyal to Him. In this you
have done foolishly; therefore from now on you
shall have wars" (2 Chronicles 16:9 NKJV).

Keep your heart tender toward God, consistently attending to the commands of Christ. You remain useful to your heavenly Father by staying sensitive to the Spirit's promptings. The Lord is not looking at your outward appearance, but at your inward integrity. Perhaps your mind needs to be cleansed from the seduction of the sensual and to be renewed with submission to the Spirit. Keep your pride in check with humble acts of service at home.

Because the Holy Spirit seeks you out, you are wise to turn toward Him and move in His direction. Obedience to God always moves us toward God, while disobedience to God always moves us away from God. The Lord may be seeking you out to replace one of His less willing servants. So remain humble as opportunities to serve Him open up. Your added responsibilities increase your responsibility to represent Christ well. So surrender to God's search for your heart.

"Submit to God and be at peace with him;
in this way prosperity will come to you" (Job 22:21).

Heavenly Father, as You seek me out, I surrender my heart to You in obedience.

Related Readings
2 Chronicles 30:8; Isaiah 26:12; John 4:23; Philippians 3:3

76

A Personal God

❦

I trust in you, L<small>ORD</small>;
I say, "You are my God."

P<small>SALM</small> 31:14

G od is personally accessible to those who call on His name by faith. He is not aloof, but engaging. God governs the entire universe, but He takes time for those who come to Him. Your trust in Him is your ticket to a personal relationship with Providence. Trust is a bridge of belief that spans the canyon of Christlessness. When we trust Him, we are positioned to know Him. Relationship without trust is incapable of intimacy and the feeling of closeness. We remain steadfast in our faith in God even in the face of suffering, temptation, and dire circumstances. He is still our God who can be trusted in our times of trouble. Our hope in God is so strong that we do not cease to call on His name in our sorrow. When we know Him, we trust Him.

Adversity and challenges, great or small, test our trust in God. Sometimes we are tempted to give up. We want to re-brand God to fit our shallow beliefs. Because He is personal, we expect Him to bend toward our immature behavior. Actually, giving up can be a good idea if we are giving up on our own solutions. But we cannot give up on God.

Christians will sometimes let us down, but Jesus never will. Christ's care is personal and persevering. He is not going anywhere. Our anger may cause us to retreat from the tender touch of our Lord, but He patiently waits for us to come back to our senses and back to Him. Don't project your dysfunctions onto Jesus. Instead, ask Him to make you a reflection of His grace, mercy, forgiveness, peace, and holiness. Get personal with your God. You can laugh with the Lord and cry with Christ. You take on the attributes of those with whom you are personal.

He is "our God" in the sense that we belong to Him. We do not own the Almighty, but sometimes we act as if we do. We make decisions and then ask Him to bless our mess. Or we don't make decisions and ask Him to bless our irresponsibility. Trying to manage our Master isn't healthy and doesn't work. Our role is not to change God and others so our lives will be better. Our role is to surrender to our Savior Jesus, asking Him to change us. We are in a personal relationship with Christ so we can reflect His ownership of our lives.

He is "our God" in the same way that a person is our mayor, our governor, or our president. We are under their authority, and God is our ultimate authority. Our rights are restricted to what God says is right.

Therefore, avoid mistrust and embrace trust in the Lord. Doubt leads to death, but trust leads to life. When you don't know what to pray, ask God to align your heart with His so your desires will become His desires. This is the best outcome of our personal prayers. Intimacy with the Almighty leads to alignment with Him. God gives us access so we can understand and apply His principles and cooperate with His purposes. So do not shun seeking out your Savior. He can be trusted. He is your God for His glory.

"Surely God is my salvation;
    I will trust and not be afraid.
The Lord, the Lord himself, is my strength
        and my defense;
    he has become my salvation" (Isaiah 12:2).

Heavenly Father, thank You for my personal salvation in Jesus and for His attention to what's best for me.

Related Readings
Psalms 31:14; 40:3; Isaiah 43:10; Habakkuk 3:18; Luke 1:47; Titus 1:4

77

A Personal Savior

The Lord is my shepherd, I lack nothing.

Psalm 23:1

A good shepherd knows his sheep up close and personal. He is committed to care for their needs and protect their interests. A loving shepherd longs to be with his sheep, to know and understand them, and to care for them the best he can. His individual and personal attention provides security for them. A caring shepherd brings his sheep peace.

In a similar way, Jesus Christ shepherds the souls of His sheep. The Lord is large and in charge, but He also knows the names and feels the emotions of His followers. He is the Great Shepherd, ruling over the entire world, and He is also the Good Shepherd, watching over individual hearts. The Lord personally shepherds saved souls with patient love. He knows His sheep, and His sheep know Him.

"You are my sheep, the sheep of my pasture, and I am your God, declares the Sovereign Lord" (Ezekiel 34:31).

Is the Lord my Shepherd? By faith, have I entered into a personal relationship with my God? Or am I a lone sheep that has wandered from the flock of faith? If He is not your Shepherd, or if you have drifted away, your Savior Jesus is waiting to bring you into the fold of His faithfulness. Let the Lord lift you onto His secure shoulders and carry you into His caring community. To survive, sheep need each other and a trustworthy shepherd. Jesus saves us from sin.

"We all, like sheep, have gone astray,
    each of us has turned to our own way;
and the Lord has laid on him
    the iniquity of us all" (Isaiah 53:6).

There are no healthy desires your Shepherd does not fulfill. Do you need forgiveness? He forgives you. Do you long for love? He loves you. Do you wish not to worry? He gives you peace. Are you afraid? He protects you. Are you confused? He clarifies with godly counsel and with His holy Word, the Bible. Are you alone? He walks with you forever.

—◦◦◦—

"I am the good shepherd; I know my sheep and
    my sheep know me—just as the Father knows
    me and I know the Father—and I lay down
        my life for the sheep" (John 10:14-15).

Therefore, listen intently to the voice of your sensitive Shepherd Jesus. He longs to lead you along His providential path. There will be tests and unknowns along the way, but fear only God and rest in His reassuring presence. He will lead you to His best, to the destination He has determined for you. Follow your Shepherd and your personal Savior Jesus.

—◦◦◦—

"The miracles I do in my Father's name speak for
    me, but you do not believe because you are not
    my sheep. My sheep listen to my voice; I know
        them, and they follow me" (John 10:25-27).

Is Jesus my personal Savior? Do I trust and follow Him as the Shepherd over my life?

Related Readings
Psalm 100:3; Ezekiel 34:11-15; Romans 8:35-37; 1 Peter 2:25

78

Personal Peace

---∞∞∞---

*In Christ Jesus you who once were far away
have been brought near by the blood of
Christ. For he himself is our peace.*

EPHESIANS 2:13-14

Jesus Christ is a personal Savior who brings a personal peace. One of the advantages of knowing Jesus is knowing His peace—a peace that passes all understanding. A person outside the kingdom of God is vulnerable to the unsettling elements of evil that prevent peace. Indeed, personal peace is a by-product of personally engaging God.

Are you at peace in your life in general and in your work in particular? If not, submit to the Prince of Peace (Jesus) and allow Him to shepherd you through your valley of trepidation. You may not know what the future holds, but you know who holds the future. Christ is our peace, so do not overlook His presence, which already resides in your heart by faith.

---∞∞∞---

"Submit to God and be at peace with him;
in this way prosperity will come to you" (Job 22:21).

Once we were far off, without faith, and in fear, but now we have been brought near to God through our belief in His Son's blood, spilled for the payment of our sins. Salvation in Jesus is a peaceful position for all who appropriate their role as children of God. When we try to substitute the peace of God with the shallow promises of the world, we only become anxious.

Your heavenly Father promises you peace in His Son Jesus. There is no need to go any further than faith in Him. Yes, peace can be elusive within an alluring and noisy culture, but Christ is at peace in you. Unfair family members may cause you to fret, and an unreasonable boss may cause you to sweat, but in the sanctuary of your soul there is peace. So don't substitute faith in Christ with a false peace. Instead, rest in His promise.

"I will listen to what God the LORD says;
    he promises peace to his people, his faithful servants—
but let them not turn to folly" (Psalm 85:8).

As you rock your feverish little one to sleep, lean into the Lord's peace. When your mind races in frantic worry, resolve in your heart that the promise of God's peace is irrevocable. When the stock market dives in uncertainty, dive deeper into the security of your Savior Jesus. Personal peace is a product of being with the One who is peace. Your Prince of Peace awaits to escort you into the calm courts of His presence.

"You know the message God sent to the people of
Israel, announcing the good news of peace through
Jesus Christ, who is Lord of all" (Acts 10:36).

In what area of my life do I need peace of mind from the Prince of Peace?

Related Readings
2 Chronicles 20:30; Isaiah 9:6; Romans 15:13,33; 1 Corinthians 14:33

79

Conflict Resolution

━━━━━⊗○○━━━━━

*If your brother or sister sins, go and point out
their fault, just between the two of you. If they
listen to you, you have won them over.*

MATTHEW 18:15

Christians tend to skirt conflict. Some perceive it as unspiritual, but Jesus teaches it is spiritual. Healthy conflict is necessary for relational and spiritual growth. It is required to keep clean accounts with others and stay focused on kingdom priorities. Conflict resolution can be uncomfortable, but if ignored, it can become ugly and even explosive.

There are two roles in the beginning stages of conflict resolution—the confronter and the receiver. If you are the confronter, it is critical to communicate the facts of the situation. If you are loose with the truth and cavalier in your confrontation, the situation will worsen, so make sure to verify and document the details.

The second critical task of the confronter is to guide the spirit of the conversation. Do not allow an accusatory tone to enter your voice. You are there in a spirit of reconciliation and healing. Avoid a condescending attitude, as you are a potential candidate for the same concerns you are bringing to your friend. Confront with a spirit of humility and grace. Speak the truth in love.

━━━━━⊗○○━━━━━

"Brothers and sisters, if someone is caught in
a sin, you who live by the Spirit should restore
that person gently. But watch yourselves, or
you also may be tempted" (Galatians 6:1).

If, on the other hand, you are the receiver, beware of defensiveness, denial, and defiance. When you are confronted, listen carefully and do not interrupt with petty excuses. After hearing out the accuser, you can correct any misconceptions and inaccuracies with a mature and level-headed spirit.

If you are the receiver, you will usually need to apologize. Nine times out of ten, your sincere apology will remedy the situation. On the other hand, a combative response will just escalate the debate into a stalemate. It is better to lose an argument and win a relationship. Treat each other as God does, and everyone wins.

If there is not a private resolution, consider the option of mediation. Mediation can involve one or two additional people. If two more are invited, each party can select one person who is respected by all. Everyone one should agree that the conclusion of the mediator(s) is the final word.

To engage with another is to care. To ignore—or worse, to gossip about another—is betrayal. The mature follower of Christ seeks to lovingly warn others of the consequences of unwise decisions. When you take the time to confront another, you could save them from embarrassment and humiliation. Grace gives an opportunity for change. Praise God for those who have done the same for us. We need each other. Confrontation now precludes more difficult confrontation later. Diffuse the conflict bomb now and avoid an explosion of egos later.

"Wounds from a friend can be trusted,
    but an enemy multiplies kisses" (Proverbs 27:6).

Whom do I need to lovingly confront over a concern because I care for them?

Related Readings
Genesis 21:25; Job 6:24; Mark 8:33; Galatians 2:11-13

80

Conflicting Loyalties

———⌇———

*By faith Moses, when he had grown up, refused
to be known as the son of Pharaoh's daughter. He
chose to be mistreated along with the people of God
rather than to enjoy the fleeting pleasures of sin.*

Sometimes we have to choose between conflicting loyalties. In some of those instances, either way we go we will disappoint, offend, or anger another party. Even more difficult, we may be loyal for years to a job or church, but then the Spirit can begin leading us in a different direction. When loyalty to our faith or family collides with competing circumstances or opportunities, we have to courageously make the choice that honors our highest priorities.

Most loyalties have their limitations. Moses struggled with the pressure to please everyone. His adoptive parents expected him to take on the regalia of royalty, but his biological family desperately needed his leadership. He would become a prince, or he would be a slave. He would wield power, or he would suffer disgrace. He would be rich, or he would be penniless. He would enjoy the pleasures of sin, or he would struggle to follow God. By faith, Moses walked away from the path of prestige for the sake of Christ. Loyalty to the Lord looks for His reward.

———⌇———

"So do not throw away your confidence; it will be
richly rewarded. You need to persevere so that
when you have done the will of God, you will receive
what he has promised" (Hebrews 10:35-36).

Are you halting between two opinions? Do you feel pulled in different directions? If so, trust God to lead you in the right way. The pain of letting down a strong personality (such as your pastor or your boss) is mild compared to the pain of disappointing those who love you the most. Your definition of loyalty may be different from your pastor's or boss's viewpoint. What matters most is your loyalty to the Lord and your loved ones. Most of all, trust your ever loyal Savior Jesus to see you through.

We are committed to remain loyal in our marriage. We persevere through pending problems, for there is a promised land from God that awaits us. Loyalty to our spouse supersedes loyalty to our parents. We honor our parents in the process, but we don't allow the lines of marriage loyalty to blur. When we weather all kinds of storms together, we better appreciate the sunshine and blessings of growing old together. Loyalty to God means loyalty to our vows. So conflicting loyalties provide us with opportunities to love the Lord. By faith, we give up sin's pleasure for His pleasure.

―――∞―――

"When the LORD takes pleasure in anyone's way,
he causes their enemies to make peace with them"
(Proverbs 16:7).

Heavenly Father, as I struggle with conflicting loyalties, help me to make choices that honor You first.

Related Readings

Exodus 2; Ruth 1:16; Haggai 1:8-9; Matthew 6:24; 10:37; Luke 14:33

81

Respond, Don't React

A gentle answer turns away wrath,
but a harsh word stirs up anger.

Proverbs 15:1

A reaction is an immediate reflex based on emotions. People react in anger when they feel insulted. They react by withdrawing when they feel left out. They react with gossip when they feel mistreated. They react defensively when they feel criticized. Reactions seem natural because they are base behaviors that operate without boundaries. A hasty reaction happens in the moment and many times leads to regret. The flesh reacts, but the Spirit leads us to respond.

A measured response, on the other hand, delays its interaction. It is based on the intellect and processed in prayer. So when we receive an email that provokes our pride or hurts our feelings, we refrain from firing back an immediate defense. We remind ourselves that email is helpful for information but less effective for true communication. When a friend or family member makes a disrespectful remark about us at a social gathering, we wait several days before talking with them so we can respond with logic, not emotion. We discuss with them how to keep our relationship whole, not fractured.

"By long forbearance and calmness of spirit a judge
or ruler is persuaded, and soft speech breaks down
the most bonelike resistance" (Proverbs 25:15 AMP).

So when your blood pressure rises, pause and ask Christ to guard your heart with His peace. When your mind goes to a worst-case scenario, ask the Lord to renew your thinking so you can see His bigger picture at work. When your throat dries and your lips are parched, let the Holy Spirit lubricate your speech with grace. When the hairs stand up on your arm, remember your heavenly Father knows the number of hairs on your head, so He can handle this event or person. Another's arrogance is agitating, but your humble response invites a calm conversation. Respond in love.

Jesus modeled a loving response in place of an angry reaction (John 7:20-24). A crowd accused Him of being demon-possessed, but instead of insulting their ignorance, He appealed to their intellect by invoking their knowledge of Moses. He went on to logically explain why it's okay to heal a broken body on the Sabbath. Indeed, Christ in us calms our spirit so we can respond rationally and respectfully. Our Spirit-led response will bear spiritual fruit. The Lord will use our soft answer to soften a heart in need of a Savior. We pray the other person will respond to Jesus in saving faith.

"Do not let any unwholesome talk come out of
your mouths, but only what is helpful for building
others up according to their needs, that it may
benefit those who listen" (Ephesians 4:29).

Heavenly Father, give me pause to respond with respect and love, not in hasty judgment.

Related Readings

Ecclesiastes 10:4; Matthew 12:36; Ephesians 5:4; Colossians 3:8

82

Processing Grief

⸺∞⸺

But you, God, see the trouble of the afflicted;
you consider their grief and take it in hand.
The victims commit themselves to you;
you are the helper of the fatherless.

PSALM 10:14

Grief is a God-given emotion that processes sorrow related to a loss. It can be the loss of a loved one to death or the death of a vision. Loss associated with finances, health, a pet, a job, divorce, or relocation contributes to extended sorrow. Nations grieve corporately over war, mass murder by a maniac, or the death of a revered national leader. Grief calls for a pause to pray and reflect on what's important. Sorrow seeks out a Savior.

Heaven's desire is to fill the hole in our hearts with hope. Sorrow slows us down, so we can use that to our advantage by meditating on what really matters—Jesus, family, and friends; spiritual, physical, and emotional health; church, fellowship, and evangelism; discipleship and God's game plan for our lives. Let your grief get you to God so you can take Him seriously. The spiritually serious are eventually able to smile. Our mourning turns into trust in Christ, and He is able to restore our joy and hope.

⸺∞⸺

"Have I not wept for those in trouble?
Has not my soul grieved for the poor?" (Job 30:25).

In addition, we can experience grief indirectly as we identify with those who have suffered great loss. Perhaps our heart aches over the atrocities caused by extreme poverty as masses are exposed to disease and ravished by malnutrition. Those who seek to live off a dollar a day have no promise of tomorrow. It is good for God's people to get worked up over those who need work. We grieve so that those of us who have received comfort in Christ will in turn comfort and serve those stuck in sorrow.

Ultimately, you have the privilege to point hurting people to their Savior Jesus. Aching souls need Almighty God to bind up their broken spirits and heal their bleeding hearts. You are heaven's vessel of hope, grace, and love. Use other people's losses to lovingly lead them to their Lord. Their loss is God's gain. What their anguish empties, faith fills. Serve their emotional and physical needs so they will embrace their spiritual needs. Grief needs God.

———⁂———

"My eyes are dim with grief.
I call to You, LORD, every day;
    I spread out my hands to You" (Psalm 88:9).

Heavenly Father, I need You to fill my heart with hope as I grieve this great loss.

Related Readings
Psalm 31:9; Proverbs 14:13; John 16:5-7,20-22; 1 Peter 1:6

83

Rest from Work

∞

There remains, then, a Sabbath-rest for the people of God; for anyone who enters God's rest also rests from their works, just as God did from his. Let us, therefore, make every effort to enter that rest, so that no one will perish by following their example of disobedience.

HEBREWS 4:9-11

For some people, resting is hard work. They love their regular job—they enjoy it and may even worship it. Hard, smart, and productive work is good, but worshipping work is bad. It is reckless and leads to ruin. It may be relational ruin, physical ruin, or even financial ruin.

Work that is worshipped gets out of hand quickly. God is the only one who deserves worship. Pride in your work can be healthy—with a pure motivation to produce quality results—but do not allow work to become an end in itself. Your true identity does not come from work. If it does, you are positioned for a roller-coaster ride of emotion. One day you will feel secure, and the next day you will be swept away by insecurity.

You are a follower of Christ, so find your identity in Him. This is one reason why rest from work is vital. When you work all the time, you tend to drift from your moorings of faith in Christ to faith in yourself. It becomes a trust issue. "Can God be trusted enough for me to rest from my work?" Of course He can. He can handle the work that remains. He divinely redeems the time of your limited work and produces results that will last longer than if you had worked all the time. After all, you are His workmanship in Christ Jesus. When you take the time to cease working, God is allowed to accelerate His work in you. Some of God's best work takes place when you don't work. He works better when you don't. His work is a work of grace, and it is a beautiful sight to behold. So enjoy your Sabbath rest as He works on your heart.

Allow Him to draw you to Himself so that when you go back to work, you are refreshed and revitalized.

As you take a break from work and enter into God's Sabbath rest, avoid the trap of resting physically but not mentally. Free your mind from this split-focused activity. Do not make your mind jealous over your body's freedom from work. Rest your thoughts from work, and you will discover your thinking is more robust and innovative when you reengage in your work. During your Sabbath rest, shift your thinking to the bigger thoughts of God and His plan. Superimpose simple faith in Him over the complex issues that are assaulting your rest.

Refresh your mind, body, and emotions during your Sabbath rest. If you are with other people during your Sabbath rest from work, relate to them with relevance and relationship. Let them see the sincerity of your focused presence. Don't act as if you wish you were somewhere else. Your rest is a time for you to relate the ways of God to others. Your life is a testament to God's faithfulness. Let others read it up close and personal. Your Sabbath rest can be a catalyst for others to reengage with God. Set the example and watch others follow. Your Sabbath rest gives others permission to do the same.

Arriving at God's rest is not always easy, but once you do, it is well worth the effort. His rest ignites your obedience and trust. So rest from work and rest in Him. Then watch your work become better.

———— ∞ ————

"God blessed the seventh day and made it
holy, because on it he rested from all the work
of creating that he had done" (Genesis 2:3).

Heavenly Father, I trust You to fill in the gaps when I take time to rest.

Related Readings

Exodus 31:15; Ecclesiastes 2:23; Luke 23:56; Hebrews 4:3

84

Forced Rest

He makes me lie down in green pastures,
he leads me beside quiet waters.

PSALM 23:2

Sometimes the Lord makes His children create margin in their lives. He understands that a life without real rest can become graceless and grumpy. Enforced margin may result from physical illness, emotional overload, spiritual fatigue, or ruptured relationships screaming for attention. The flesh thinks it can continue with little or no rest, but the spirit knows better.

We may work through our fatigue and fake it for a while, but eventually we hit an unscalable wall with nothing more to give. Jesus knows we are extra vulnerable during these tired times, and He makes a way of retreat and rest. His gentle and loving care calls us to come away with Him. It's much better to heed His invitation for intimacy than to move down the road without Him. Resting in the Lord invigorates and inspires.

We can spare ourselves discomfort by choosing to rest rather than waiting for our Master to force us to take a break. A wise man understands the need for rhythms of rest in his schedule. This is why a good night's sleep and occasional naps are necessary. Weekends, especially Sundays, are made for rest, reflection, and rejuvenation. If we are intoxicated by activity, we run the risk of living in a restless hangover. Real rest allows us to recover and unwind in God's presence.

Just as green pastures are pleasant and fulfilling for any animal that depends on the earth, God's heavenly resources feed our souls, fill our minds, and hydrate our hearts. Are you tired and overwhelmed? Do you feel alone and depleted of any energy to engage with others? If so, take the time to get away with God. Say no to the unnecessary and yes to the necessary. The most productive people accomplish more by doing less. They rest in Him.

Most importantly, allow the Lord to lead you by faith into a quiet place. Sit by the soothing silence of still waters and drink in the majesty of God's creation. You know Jesus is leading you when you intentionally engage in solitude for the purpose of hearing His voice. Lie on His green grass and look up so your gaze is on God. Don't resist the rest you require. Instead, cease and desist your activity and embrace and celebrate His rest. The grandeur of God's glory comes down to care for you.

"When I consider your heavens,
    the work of your fingers,
the moon and the stars,
    which you have set in place,
what is mankind that you are mindful of them,
    human beings that you care for them?" (Psalm 8:3-4).

Do I voluntarily engage with eternity in quiet places? Does my life rhythm include rest?

Related Readings

Exodus 31:13; 2 Samuel 22:33-34; Zechariah 10:1; Romans 9:11

85

Humbled by Ill-Health

———— ∞ ————

*Naaman's servants went to him and said, "My father, if
the prophet had told you to do some great thing, would
you not have done it? How much more, then, when
he tells you, 'Wash and be cleansed'!" So he went
down and dipped himself in the Jordan seven times,
as the man of God had told him, and his flesh was
restored and became clean like that of a young boy.*

2 KINGS 5:13-14

Our hearts are softened when sickness seizes our bodies. A sensitivity and tenderness of heart that lay dormant may finally appear in the behavior of a controlling Christian. When a body is under fire from illness, it could be asking the soul to release control and cling to Christ. At first there may be an angry reaction, but eventually the will succumbs to a sense that God's got it covered—He is in control. Faith in the face of fiery trials is the fruit of humility. Sickness is an invitation to submit to Jesus.

When our lives are smothered by clouds of uncertainty, we find opportunities to engage in acts of obedience. As we walk in humility, we listen for the Lord's voice. He speaks through His Word and His Spirit, His teachers and preachers, His children, and experts in treating physical ailments. Prayer and modern medicine create a powerful partnership in producing positive outcomes. A humbled heart creates clarity of mind for wisdom in decision making. Humility invites healing.

———— ∞ ————

"Jesus reached out his hand and touched
the man. 'I am willing,' he said. 'Be clean!'
And immediately the leprosy left him.

"Then Jesus ordered him, 'Don't tell anyone,

> but go, show yourself to the priest and offer
> the sacrifices that Moses commanded for
> your cleansing, as a testimony to them.'
>
> "Yet the news about him spread all the more, so
> that crowds of people came to hear him and to
> be healed of their sicknesses" (Luke 5:13-15).

Your cure may very well be different from another suffering saint's cure. Mysteriously, your body may respond well to certain treatments while someone in a similar condition experiences a totally different result. So you pray, research, and trust the Spirit to lead you in the Lord's plan for your body. Don't miss the holistic approach of healing in your body, mind, will, emotions, and spirit. Humility is the gateway to God's grace and wholeness.

Allow the Lord to use health issues to bring vulnerability and intimacy into your relationships. Be real about your fears and ill feelings. Allow friends to comfort you. Emotional awareness and engagement are healthy outcomes of a humbled heart. Renew your mind daily with the truth of Scripture and bend your will toward your biblical beliefs. Physical health is good, but spiritual wholeness is best. A humbled heart hears the Lord.

> "LORD, do not forsake me;
>   do not be far from me, my God.
> Come quickly to help me,
>   my Lord and my Savior" (Psalm 38:21-22).

Heavenly Father, I humble my heart so I can hear from You and be healed.

Related Readings
Job 14:22; Psalm 38:6-8; Proverbs 17:22; Mark 7:37; 3 John 2

86

Healthy Nourishment

*At the end of the ten days they looked healthier
and better nourished than any of the young
men who ate the royal food. So the guard took
away their choice food and the wine they were
to drink and gave them vegetables instead.*

DANIEL 1:15-16

God wants His children to be good stewards of their bodies. The Creator of the body has defined dietary guidelines that have proven to be beneficial to physical health. Who would know better what to put into the mouth and ingest into the stomach than the One who made us? The original designer of an all-natural diet is the One who commands fruits, nuts, and vegetables to grow. A return to natural food is a return to the way the Lord expects us to steward the bodies He has given us.

In our youth, many of us had the physical capacity to eat a greater variety and quantity of food. However, as we grow older and gain wisdom (and weight!) we can make more educated food choices. Safe to say, whatever our stage of life, we are smart to be selective in what and how much we eat. Normally if we plan a menu in advance and dine at home, we have more control over our consumption of calories and nutrition.

"Do you not know that your bodies are temples of the Holy Spirit, who is in you, whom you have received from God? You are not your own; you were bought at a price. Therefore honor God with your bodies" (1 Corinthians 6:19-20).

Yes, partake in your Maker's diet, and He will make you healthier than if you follow a haphazard approach to good eating. For example, focus on small portions of lean protein, such as beef, chicken, or fish, accompanied by a fresh salad, vegetables, and fruit. God may call you to be a vegetarian for a season to slow down your intake of meat. Temperance tames your appetite. But be cautious—food obsessions can make the menu an idol. Start by simply consuming small amounts of fresh food. When you manage well the Holy Spirit's temple (your body), you manage to feel better.

Limit the intake of beverages other than water. Any excessive drinking of soda, alcohol, coffee, tea, or juice will add too many calories, eventually contributing to obesity and disease. Liquid calories and nutritional values should be monitored with equal resolve as solid. In addition, keep an eye on your intake of sugar and sodium, as they are two unhealthy culprits at restaurants. Most of all, see yourself as a wise physical manager of your Creator's body. Check out God's specific guidelines in Leviticus 11 and Acts 10:9-16. Be like Daniel—keep your appetites under the Spirit's control so others will take notice and ask you why.

"Worship the LORD your God, and his blessing will
be on your food and water" (Exodus 23:25).

Heavenly Father, I am grateful to You for creating my body. I want to follow Your guidelines for healthy eating.

Related Readings

Deuteronomy 28:1-14; Leviticus 11; Malachi 2:15; Acts 10:9-16;
    1 Corinthians 6:13

87

Emotional Health

⎯⎯⎯ ◠◦◠ ⎯⎯⎯

Above all else, guard your heart,
for everything you do flows from it.

PROVERBS 4:23

The condition of our hearts is an indicator of our emotional health. A wounded heart limps along, vulnerable to fatigue and frustration, while a healed heart can resist the wiles of the world. Healthy emotions heal. A strong heart has access to an abundance of grace, so its capacity to offer forgiveness and exercise patience is vast. Yes, the grace of God gives emotional health to all who engage it. When emotions are in good shape, we are in sync with the Spirit.

Just as we care for our physical health, so must we manage our emotional well-being. Checkups of the soul with a mature Jesus follower increase our understanding of where we stand. The expertise of a trusted spiritual advisor is necessary for us to be objective in our own emotional assessment. Just as physical trainers show us how to keep our bodies healthy with a balance of weights and cardio, so spiritual trainers give us insight in how to express our feelings and forgive personal offenses.

⎯⎯⎯ ◠◦◠ ⎯⎯⎯

"A good man brings good things out of the good
stored up in his heart, and an evil man brings evil
things out of the evil stored up in his heart. For the
mouth speaks what the heart is full of " (Luke 6:45).

The Holy Spirit is the best manager of our emotions. Just as a successful coach leads a team to work together to win, so the Spirit leads our emotions to work together for God's glory. When our emotions are under the influence of the Holy Spirit, we walk in wholeness and holiness. Emotional health happens when our feelings are filtered by the Spirit. He removes distasteful impurities. Indeed, a heart controlled by the Spirit is able to give life to other lives.

How's your heart? Are you keenly sensitive to the Spirit's leading, or are you overly sensitive to fleshly feelings? Have your emotional wounds healed? Are you blessed with a healthy heart? Take a risk and be vulnerable about your past hurts so you can experience present healing. Surround yourself with caring Christ followers with whom you can process your feelings. Most of all, share your heart with your Savior Jesus, who will cleanse your heart, heal it, and make it whole.

"The Lord will guide you always;
    He will satisfy your needs in a sun-scorched land
    and will strengthen your frame.
You will be like a well-watered garden,
    like a spring whose waters never fail" (Isaiah 58:11).

Heavenly Father, I submit to Your Spirit—the manager and filter of my emotions.

Related Readings

2 Kings 10:31; Proverbs 10:11; John 20:22; Acts 2:33; Revelation 22:17

88

Christic Is Wisdom

∞

We preach Christ crucified: a stumbling block
to Jews and foolishness to Gentiles, but to those
whom God has called, both Jews and Greeks, Christ
the power of God and the wisdom of God.

1 CORINTHIANS 1:23-24

Christ is the wisdom of God, so to know Him is to know and understand godly wisdom. The life of Jesus illustrates wisdom for us, and His teaching educates us in wisdom. Christians are able to grow in godly wisdom when they're in relationship with God the Son. The source of wise counsel is found in Christ. Just as pure water bubbles from the crevice of a remote mountain rock, so God's living water of truth flows from the heart of Jesus.

Because wisdom starts with Jesus, our journey to becoming wise begins with a personal relationship with Christ. The Holy Scriptures declare a Savior who loves and receives all who come to Him in faith and repentance. Salvation in Jesus Christ is the first step required to obtain His wisdom. Fear of God leads to faith in God, which can then access the wisdom of God. Have you placed your faith in Jesus Christ? If so, you are very wise.

∞

"You have known the Holy Scriptures, which are
able to make you wise for salvation through
faith in Christ Jesus" (2 Timothy 3:15).

Having access to wisdom through faith in Jesus, we are then wise to lean into understanding His ways. Like a starved man coming off of a ten-day hunger strike, we can anticipate enjoying a smorgasbord of truth. Christ's wisdom is rich in relational nutrients, financial nourishment, and emotional energy. Your Savior Jesus is not stingy with His counsel—He liberally gives wisdom to those He loves.

As the personification of wisdom, Jesus unconditionally loved people. He loved rich and poor, Jew and Gentile, male and female. He loved city folks and country dwellers. The educated and uneducated felt His fierce love. Kings and commoners did not escape His all-consuming compassion. Jesus, the all-wise one, initiated conversations of wisdom wherever He went.

Who in your circle of influence is hungry for the wisdom of Christ? Whom can you love by sharing His counsel? Once you discover His freeing truth, you are responsible to pay it forward by faith to other hungry hearts. Lead people to the waters of Christ's wisdom, and they will never thirst again. You will be giving a cup of wisdom in Jesus's name, and you will show them how to draw from the deep well of His wisdom themselves. Jesus is the wisdom of God.

"Let the message of Christ dwell among you richly as you teach and admonish one another with all wisdom through psalms, hymns, and songs from the Spirit, singing to God with gratitude in your hearts" (Colossians 3:16).

What steps can I take to search the Holy Scriptures, gain Christ's wisdom, and grow to know Him better?

Related Readings
Romans 16:27; 1 Corinthians 1:30; Ephesians 1:17; Colossians 1:28

89

God Is Love

———— ∞ ————

God is love.

1 John 4:8

God's love never ceases. Christ's love is continual because it flows from the inexhaustible reservoir of God's goodness. Man's lakes can languish for lack of rain, but the Lord's never will. There is no drought of love in the divine landscape. Love rains down from heaven in sheets of mercy and faithfulness. It pelts our pride and melts our heart. The love of God endures. Your heavenly Father's love is not fickle. It is faithful and true.

Your earthly father's love may be conditional and undependable. Loving may be difficult for him because he has not been loved. But you have the opportunity and privilege of moving beyond the drought of your dad's love and bowing beneath the overflow of Christ's compassion. Christ's covenant of love with His children never alters. You can trust God's unfailing love for ever and ever (Psalm 52:8).

God's enduring love gives you a reason to rejoice. His love is your excuse to exercise enormous, ongoing praise and thanksgiving. Do not remain defeated by dire circumstances and negative thinking. God loves you—He has saved your soul. God loves you—He has made you whole. God loves you—He provides you work. God loves you—He has given you life. God loves you!

You need a full understanding of every good thing God has given you (Philemon 1:6). As that recognition grows in you, you will more freely exclaim His goodness and mercy. Your shouts of joy will drown out the murmurings meandering in your mind. You are His. "Owned by God" is your trademark of trust. Let gratitude govern your thinking because God's love endures forever.

Because His love is everlasting, you have Christ's capacity to continually love. You can love sinners and saints alike. Jesus did (Luke 5:30-31). He spent time with people unlike Himself. This is the posture of love. Make sure you share your love with the unlovable. Be patient, kind, and forgiving toward family members who don't have a clue of what Christ has done for them. Love them even when they are hard to understand. Love them in spite of their unfair criticism and surly sarcasm.

Release God's love to shine through your soul. Be a leader of love. You know better than to live any other way. Your love will make a lasting impression on your parents and on your children. The Lord uses Christ's love manifested through you to lead others to Himself. Be a leader whose love endures. Love during the good times and especially the hard times. Love endures.

───✦───

"For the Lord is good and his love endures forever;
   his faithfulness continues through all generations"
      (Psalm 100:5).

Heavenly Father, I praise You, for You are enduring love. May Your love flow through my life for Your glory!

Related Readings
Nehemiah 13:26; Psalm 36:7; 42:8; Joel 2:13; Romans 8:39;
   Ephesians 3:17-18

90

Spirit-Led Living

———— ∞ ————

So he said to me, "This is the word of the LORD
to Zerubbabel. 'Not by might nor by power, but
by my Spirit,' says the LORD Almighty."

ZECHARIAH 4:6

The Holy Spirit is God's fuel for living. He leads, convicts, com-
forts, and gives courage. On the other hand, the world promotes
power and might. The world's approach is forceful—if the door is
closed, knock it down. If you have power and authority, use them to
make things happen. This lack of faith can lead to panic and unrighteous results.

Spirit-led living is different from the way of the world. It's about
dependence on God rather than anything else. Money, might, and
power are cheap imitations of dependence on God. These temporal for-
tresses are fleeting. When all is said and done, they are undependable.
Money, control, and your title can be here today and gone tomorrow.

The Spirit of God wants you to grow in your awareness of Him and
to follow His lead. Like a hurricane as it gains strength, God's Spirit
will carry you along as you surrender to Him. You cannot accomplish
His best without the leadership and empowerment of the Holy Spirit.
He may even lead you to places of discomfort to help you learn to
depend on Him.

The Holy Spirit led Jesus to the wilderness to be tempted by Satan,
but the Word of God became Christ's defense. He deflected the darts of
the devil with the truth of God. His exercise of faith and obedience drew
Him closer to His heavenly Father. Instead of driving Him from God,
His test drew Him to God. The Holy Spirit's goal is to get us to God.

———— ∞ ————

"Jesus said to him, 'Away from me, Satan! For it is
written: "Worship the Lord your God, and serve
him only."' Then the devil left him, and angels
came and attended him" (Matthew 4:10-11).

Submission to God revives your sensitivity to the Spirit of God.
Come under the authority of God, and you will have a source of
strength that is limitless and energizing. God's Spirit also produces
fruit and creates character. These are more benefits of Spirit-led living.
It's not about techniques and tactics. It's primarily about the character
of Christ transforming your life.

Your heart will explode with God's powerful love rather than exploit
others with threats. A quiet confidence comes from a deep abiding in
Christ. Spirit-led moms pray more than they worry. They train their
children while entrusting them to God. Anxiety is replaced with abiding. They do their part and trust God to do His part.

Spirit-led living is all about engrafting the Word of God into your
life. The Holy Spirit ignites the fuel of God's Word into a blaze of obedience. This is the power that changes lives and communities for God's
greater good. This exhibition of power may not make headlines here,
but heaven will take notice. Wait on God, be Spirit-led, and watch His
power prevail!

"The Spirit gives life; the flesh counts for
nothing. The words I have spoken to you—they
are full of the Spirit and life" (John 6:63).

Where is the Holy Spirit leading me that requires uncommon
faith and obedience?

Related Readings
Exodus 31:3; John 3:34; Acts 4:25-31; 2 Timothy 1:7

Acknowledgments

Thank you, James Isbill, for being a father-in-law who models how to love family better than anyone I know. Your energy for life and for loving your wife and children molded me into the husband and father I have become. To George Bailey, for being a man who worked diligently and who worked smart. I am grateful to you for instilling your work ethic into me, your son. To Mitch and Jim, for being brothers who love me with your respect and friendship. To Timmy Isbill, for being a brother-in-law who loves people as well as anyone I know (thank you especially for asking me to skate with your sister Rita in seventh grade on her birthday!).

Thank you to the men who have been examples and mentors for me. To Richard Ferguson, for being a high school football coach who modeled gentle toughness to a very impressionable teenager. Most of all, thanks for pointing me to Jesus. To Danny McCarra, for taking me fishing, and Fred Hopper, for taking me hunting. To Bob McDonald, for igniting my entrepreneurial spirit as a young man.

Thank you to James Sammons for mentoring me as a young seminarian. To Dan Grindstaff, for being a friend when I was a very insecure minister. To Lynn Madden, for taking me under wing in my first church out of seminary. To Nolen Rollins, for mentoring me in administrative details and organization. To Steve Reed, for mentoring me for seven intense years. To Howard Dayto, for mentoring me in humility and prayer. To Jess Correll, for mentoring me in generosity, big vision, and action.

Thanks to my accountability group of ten years: Mike Kendrick, Woody Faulk, Joel Manby, and Lanny Donoho. To the men in our couples small group of four years who know the good, the bad, and the ugly about me and still love me: Bill Ibsen, Andy Ward, Josh Randolph, and Bill Chapman. To Kevin Latty and Larry Green, for following

God's call to start the men's retreat Souly Business and for the way it has challenged and grown my manhood.

Thank you to the First Southern Bank of Kentucky and your incredible encouragement over the years to write devotionals: Jess Correll, Doug Ditto, Tommy Roberts, Rusty Clark, John Ball, Mike Taylor, Dan Lewis, and Jimmy Rousey.

Thank you to the Ministry Ventures board: Woody Faulk, Mark Peebles, Mark Pighini, David Deeter, Larry Green, Alan Gotthardt, Chris Bledsoe, and Adam Strange. To the Ministry Ventures board of influencers: Paul Masters, Bob Kilinski, David McKinnon, Danny Philips, John Flack, Kevin Latty, Jeff Stott, Gary Young, Ida Bell, David Ward, Jerry Lindaman, and Greg Adams. And to the Ministry Ventures staff team: Jon Bennett, Beth Bennett, Mike Flink, Josh Randolph, Melodie Stroligize, Cindy McDaniel, James Fillingame, Michael Johnson, and Arnold Kimmons.

Thank you to the Wisdom Hunters board: Deb Ochs, John Hightower, Andrew Weller, Cliff Bartow, Scott Melby, and Jack McEntee. To the Wisdom Hunters staff team: Bethany Thoms, Rita Bailey, Susan Fox, Rachel Snead, Rachel Prince, and Gwynne Maffett.

Thanks to my businessmen's book club: David Deeter, Nathan Deeter, and Mike Davis. And to my classics book club: Bill Ibsen, Bill Williams, and Larry Green. Thank you to Suzy Grey (on loan from Andy Stanley—thanks, Andy!) for shepherding this project as a meticulous book agent with thoroughness and always with a smile. Thank you to Perry McGuire for your detailed work on trademarking Two Minutes in the Bible! And a very big shout-out to the incredible team at Harvest House Publishers, including Bob Hawkins, Shane White, Gene Skinner, Kathy Zemper, Pat Mathis, and Mary Cooper!

Most of all, thanks to my heavenly Father for loving me unconditionally—tough and tender.

About the Author

Boyd Bailey enjoys the role of chief encouragement officer at Ministry Ventures, a company he cofounded in 1999. His passion is to encourage and equip leaders engaged in kingdom-focused enterprises. Since 2004 he has also served as president and founder of Wisdom Hunters, a ministry that connects people to Christ through devotional writing—with more than 100,000 daily email readers.

Ministry Ventures has trained approximately 1000 faith-based nonprofits and coached for certification more than 200 ministries in the best practices of prayer, board development, ministry models, administration, and fundraising. By God's grace, these ministries have raised more than $100 million, and thousands of people have been led into growing relationships with Jesus Christ.

Prior to Ministry Ventures, Boyd was the national director for Crown Financial Ministries. He was instrumental in the expansion of Crown into 30 major markets across the United States. He was a key facilitator in the $25 million merger between Christian Financial Concepts and Crown Ministries.

Before Boyd's work with Crown, he and Andy Stanley started First Baptist Atlanta's north campus, and as an elder, Boyd assisted Andy in the start of North Point Community Church.

Boyd received a bachelor of arts from Jacksonville State University and a masters of divinity from Southwestern Seminary in Fort Worth, Texas. Boyd and his wife, Rita, live in Roswell, Georgia. They have been married 34 years and are blessed with four daughters, three sons-in-law, and five grandchildren.

Wisdom Hunters Resources by Boyd Bailey

Visit WisdomHunters.com to subscribe to free daily devotional emails or to choose from a wide selection of devotional books (e-book and print versions available).

Download the free Wisdom Hunters app from iTunes for a daily devotional for iPhone and iPad.

Two Minutes in the Bible™ Through Proverbs

To find practical answers for everyday challenges, you can't go wrong with the book of Proverbs. And to help you apply its timeless truth to every area of your own life, Boyd Bailey offers these concise and down-to-earth daily readings.

Building strong relationships, achieving financial stability, speaking words that help and heal...you'll find God's plan for your success in all these areas and many more. Each brief devotion includes a question to help you remember the message and take appropriate action.

Start each day with just two minutes in the Bible. You'll soon be enjoying the benefits of a storehouse of wisdom in your heart.

To learn more about Harvest House books and
to read sample chapters, visit our website:

www.harvesthousepublishers.com

HARVEST HOUSE PUBLISHERS
EUGENE, OREGON